15th Floor, Concorde Building, Dinan Street, Verdun
Beirut - Lebanon P.O. Box: 14-6613

Tel: 00961 1 752 100 - Fax: 00961 1 748 555
www.tpbooksonline.com

First edition: November 2008

ISBN: 9953-0-0029-8

Printing: Dots (Dar el-Kotob)

MiSS Guided

How to step into the Lebanese glam lane

Written by: Anissa Rafeh
Illustrations: Benoit Debbane

Introduction: Michael Karam
Editing: Faerlie Wilson

Art Direction: Reem Abou Chacra Kudsi
Design and Execution: Sari Nasrallah

This book is dedicated with much love to all
the fabulous women of Lebanon.

And also to *Hanan*, the greatest Lebanese woman I
know, and *Wael*, who was smart enough to marry her.

BIOGRAPHIES

Anissa Rafeh was born to Lebanese parents in 1974 in Louisville, Kentucky. After living in Dubai from age 5 to 16, she moved back to the US with her family in 1990. She graduated from the University of Richmond in Virginia in 1995, and then moved to Lebanon to pursue a Master's degree in political science from the American University of Beirut. After graduation, she worked in journalism, enjoying a successful career as both a writer and editor. Over the years, she has had numerous articles published on a variety of topics, from the serious to the lighthearted, covering the worlds of politics, business and show business. From 2004 to 2006, she worked as the editor of *What's Up?*, a Lebanese entertainment magazine, and wrote a monthly column, *The Simple Things*, a humorous look at her experiences living in Lebanon. Anissa currently lives in Beirut, where she runs her own copywriting service, EditMax. *MissGuided* is her first book, in which she has combined her two loves: writing and Lebanon.

Benoit Debbane was born in Lebanon in 1974. He studied architecture at ALBA and is now a popular illustrator for local magazines, newspapers, advertising agencies and book publishers. He has put all this experience to good use, passing his artistic skills on to the next generation as an illustration and image editing instructor at ALBA and LAU in Beirut. Benoit loves cats, and if he had his way, one would have appeared in each of the illustrations of *MissGuided!*

FOREWORD

Jane Austen may have started it all with her dictum, "It is a truth universally acknowledged, that a single man in possession of a good fortune must be in want of a wife." *Shoo habla!* If Austen were Lebanese, she would have had the instinctive good sense to know that the truth is, in fact, that a single man in possession of a good fortune must be there to buy Dolce & Gabbana.

Austen, being the bookish sort *(ya haram)*, probably never encountered *Lebanus Waxus Brazilia,* one of the most beautiful yet temperamental of all the female species found on the planet. Anissa Rafeh's years of painstaking research were the groundwork for what is sure to be the definitive guide for all those who aspire to the high standards of modern living – not to mention survival tactics – by which this wonderful and exotic creature abides. Whether it's going on a date, wearing the right shoes or simply avoiding the amorous advances of the less evolved members of society, it's all here in this gorgeous and perfectly-formed reference.

Anissa has endured the endless coffees, lunches, dinners and matchmaking meetings with fussing aunts. She has been plucked and waxed just to see a rare sub-breed Lebanese man – *Lebanus Moronicus* – at his preening best. She has learned that there is no better form of defense than an attack and there is always a solution to the many curveballs life (or genetics) can throw at you. Got a wonky nose? Get a new one. And she exhorts women NEVER to allow either a hairy back (wax, my dear) or bad dress sense (shopping, duh!) to stand in the way of an advantageous love match. Did Jane Austen tell us this? *A-ba-dan!*

Michael Karam is one of Lebanon's most popular journalists and an award-winning wine writer. His real claim to fame however is that he is the co-author of *Life's Like That!* and *Life's Even More Like That!* (both by Turning Point), two volumes of caricatures that take a light-hearted look at the Lebanese and their way of life.

ACKNOWLEDGEMENTS

There are many people I need to thank for their invaluable help while I was writing this book. First, I extend much appreciation to my friend, Michael Karam, for taking the time to write the foreword. I also need to thank professional wine consultant, Paul Koder, from Wine Trend, Inc., for his help with pairing wines and chocolate. Many thanks also go to nutritionist and dietician Nadeen Massaad, who kindly provided the calorie counter on popular Lebanese food. I'm also grateful to journalist Mona Alami, who graciously allowed me to use some of her research.

I am also indebted to my close friends and family, who took the time to read this book and offer constructive feedback, not to mention a great deal of encouragement – most especially, my parents and my sisters, Kinda, Alyah and Nadya as well as my brother, Adam.

And finally, I would like to thank Charlotte Hamaoui and Eleena Sarkissian from Turning Point – first, for their insight to take on this project to begin with, and second, for their unfailing support during the entire process of writing *MissGuided*.

CONTENTS

Chapter I
Vanity Affair

Mirror, mirror on the wall...

Oh, the things Lebanese women do to get beautiful! It may look effortless, but don't be fooled – it takes an army to get them primped and primed for public viewing. In fact, to call the typical gal in Beirut 'vain' would be an understatement – she would not even consider going out on the street without being fully made up from head to toe, even if she's just hopping over to the supermarket to buy hair conditioner. But, to get glam and fabulous *à la Libanaise*, you must have the four essentials: a good hairstylist, manicurist, eyebrow shaper and plastic surgeon. Forget earth, air, water and fire, the elements of beauty are all you need to become a member of the elite 'hot' club. Let the grooming begin!

MANE game

The crowning glory of any female, a woman's hair is her foremost tool for attracting the opposite sex, which is why you will find a salon on virtually every street corner from Beirut to even the most rural village in the far reaches of Lebanon.

Lebanese women never leave the house unless **perfectly coiffed** so if you don't want to look like a homeless person in comparison, be sure to get your hair done once to twice a week.

For everyday, you should always go for 'lisse,' or straight, sleek locks. God forbid you go out in public with your naturally curly or wavy tresses, even if it means you forgo washing your hair in between 'brushings' (blow dries).

There really is no excuse for not having a beautiful 'do at all times, especially since it only takes about 20 minutes to get your hair picture perfect. Plus, depending on where you go, a brushing can cost as little as under $4 (keep that secret) to $20 (shout it out from the rooftops). Although getting a blow dry at any salon is acceptable, getting it cut at a lesser-known place is most definitely not.

When people ask you where you do your hair, you absolutely must be able to name one of the swankier salons in the city, preferably one known to be frequented by at least one of the rich and famous.

Yes, even your hair can get a bad reputation in this town!

As for the color of your hair, *au naturel* is definitely not an option. In fact, virgin hair is a rare phenomenon that probably hasn't been seen since the Romans built Baalbeck. In this country, there are several staple colors that pretty much everyone sports, give or take a tint or two. If you're going for the 'I could be from Scandinavia… Not' look, be sure to go for blond highlights. Those enamored with songbird Haifa Wehbe will undoubtedly opt for the jet black strands she made popular – just be sure to complete the look with shining blue contact lenses and thick black eyeliner (surgical enhancements optional). Then there are the cyclical hits, like bright red and eggplant – who knows when these favorites will be back in style, but let's hope not anytime soon because let's face it, no one wants to look like they're wearing a wilting vegetable on their head.

Don't worry about whether or not you look natural, as long as your hairstyle follows the current trend and is deemed fashionable, then all basic requirements have been met and all's right with the world – until the next 'in' look comes along, that is.

The nail files and ALL THE TRIMMINGS

Being well manicured is just as important as being well coiffed, so getting your nails done is an absolute must. In the winter, you can get away with unpedicured toes, but painted fingernails are a year-round obligation. The Lebanese love affair of all things French continues with nails, with the French manicure – are you really surprised? – being arguably the most popular style.

When it comes to length, remember that tips should not be mistaken for bear claws, so leave the talons for the creatures of the wild. As for adding a touch of color, try not to go for anything outrageously tacky – hot pink is okay for bubble gum – unless, of course, you're okay with looking like someone who belongs in a trailer park.

The added bonus of getting a mani/pedi on a regular basis (other than looking marvelous, of course) is that most nail salons are one-stop beauty repair shops, offering everything under the sun, including cosmetic tattoos, facials and massages. So, the next time you make a nail appointment, you might as well go for all the trimmings while you're there. Although the aforementioned are optional beauty treatments for the glamorous Lebanese, one thing certainly isn't: eyebrow shaping.

Even if you're trying to channel your inner Brooke Shields, get your eyebrows done by an expert.

Try not to go for extremes though, as it is doubtful that the bushiness sported by Wolverine in the *X-Men* movies or the penciled in arched line circa 1920 is a good look for anyone. For those of you who over-plucked as a teen and are only left with a few stray tufts of hair dangling by a fragile thread on your brow, salvation is at hand: throw out that brow pencil and have them filled in permanently with a nifty tattoo job.

Speaking of cosmetic tattoo jobs, in addition to your eyebrows, you can have practically your whole face inked on. Yes, from thicker lips to everlasting eyeliner, it all can be yours, as long as you have the stamina to withstand the needle that is part and parcel of permanently etching color into your skin. If it sounds painful, that's because *it is*. Well, there is a reason they say that the price of beauty is pain.

Ouch!

A less painful, albeit mighty important, step in your beauty regimen is teeth whitening. If you can't get it taken care of at your local beauty salon, any dentist will be able to give your pearly whites that extra gleaming touch for a radiant smile. If the damage to your enamel is minimal, you could go for the more economical whitening strips that you can apply at home (never wear them out in public, ladies!) and which you can usually find at the pharmacy or supermarket. Just remember, though, that the objective is to highlight your smile, not make your teeth glow in the dark when the electricity goes out, so don't overdo it.

And now we have come to the end of our long day's journey along the path to beauty! After all the cutting, scraping, plucking, prodding and pricking, you are entitled to reward yourself with a relaxing massage or facial. So, unwind from the ordeal of getting gorgeous and just think of looking in the mirror and being able to declare with conviction that you are once again the fairest of them all!

Moment of ZEN

The next time you're in the mood for the ultimate pampering session, choose one of the treaments listed below to reach your moment of Zen!

TREATMENT	WHAT IT DOES
Hot stone massage	A delicious end to a stressful week, this treatment involves heated stones placed along vital energy points on your body to balance your mind, body and soul in perfect harmony.
Seaweed wrap	With seaweed wrapped around your body for about an hour, this treatment promises not only to relax you, but it will also detoxify your skin.
Chocolate body wrap	Mildly heated dark chocolate is decadently dripped over your body for about an hour as the natural cocoa enhances your skin. Yummy!
Reflexology massage	Using this ancient technique of healing by applying pressure to certain points on the body, the massage relieves tension as well as minor aches and pains.
Mud bath	It sounds messy, but your skin will benefit from all the minerals found in natural mud. A one hour dip is even said to help alleviate minor aches and pains.
Salt and oil scrub	Exfoliate with a salt rub and then luxuriate as relaxing oils are massaged into your skin.
Facial	With an array of treatments, from deep cleansing to skin firming facials, you're bound to find one suited to your skin needs.
Prenatal massage	Specifically catered to expecting moms, this massage will safely relax you using non-harmful oils and minerals.

Bring out THE PLASTIC

Fast becoming the cosmetic surgery capital of the Middle East, Lebanon is the one place where you're sure to find a bevy of babes sporting the same nose… and boobs… and lips. No, they are not *Stepford Wives*, but just surgically enhanced Lebanese women. Cosmetic procedures have in fact become so commonplace in the country that a woman with all her original parts is now an extraordinary sight. From those obsessed with finding the elusive fountain of youth to those who think that looking like a toy doll is the epitome of beauty, there is something for just about everyone in the land of plastic – surgery, that is.

Rhinoplasty is perhaps the most popular of cosmetic procedures performed here, but did you ever wonder why Lebanon has become nose job central? When exactly was the Mediterranean nose ruled a beauty catastrophe? Why is the unnaturally tiny, skinny, ski slope nose such a coveted feature even though everyone and their mother seems to have it? So many questions, so few answers. It boggles the mind that most women would die if they were at a party where someone else was wearing the same outfit, yet they have no qualms about getting the exact same nose as a big chunk of the female population.

Although when getting a new nose most choose to go smaller, for the lips and chest, it's always the bigger, the better. In both cases, though, going too big can be a huge disaster. In the first instance, getting too much collagen injected will get you comparisons to a guppy fish at best and to someone whose mouth got stuck in the pool gutter at worst. Thicker lips do not always a perfect pout make.

As for boob jobs, if your chest is hitting your chin, you'll know you've maybe gone a cup size - or three - too large.

Double-Ds only look good on porn stars, so unless you're okay with being mistaken for one, try for something a little less outrageous.

Next we come to the greatest invention of the 20th century – no, not sliced bread, but Botox! Whatever did women do before they could inject a poison to paralyze those pesky facial muscles – you know, the ones that allow you to form expressions – so that all traces of aging will be smoothed out? So what if you can no longer move your forehead or laugh, isn't trying to look an age you haven't been in decades far more important? Of course it is.

SKINTASTIC solutions

Before going under the knife, take a look at this list of the most popular non-surgical anti-aging procedures.

PROCEDURE	WHAT IT DOES
Botox	Used to temporarily rid the face of meddlesome frown lines, crows feet and forehead creases, this substance works by weakening the muscles in the injected area. It lasts for up to five months, but be prepared to lose some facial movement.
Chemical peel	This treatment removes the outer layer of the skin to get rid of fine lines. Depending on the level of the peel (from superficial to deep), the severity of the burn varies. If you're going for a light peel, it'll take about an hour and you can immediately go about your business. For a deep peel, expect your face to look raw for a couple of days.
Collagen	Used to make the lips fuller, these injections take minutes, giving you an instant pout lasting several months.
Dermabrasion & Microdermabrasion	Both techniques are used to scrape away the outer layer of skin for a smoother, rejuvenated appearance, the former being less invasive than the latter.
Fillers	These injections are used to smooth out small lines and wrinkles, particularly around the mouth. They can even be used to plump up the lips and last from six to 18 months.
Thread lift	Like its name suggests, this procedure uses string threaded through the face along specific lines in the forehead, around the eyes, cheeks, and around the mouth, which are then lifted to give the appearance of a face lift. Unlike surgery, this process only takes about 40 minutes and is completely reversible.

Hair RAISERS (for him and her)

One of the major grooming areas that is an absolute necessity for Lebanese women is body hair removal. Thankfully, there are many different methods available, from the oh-so-convenient razor to the more painful *sukkar* (sugar), waxing and laser. The razor is obviously the easiest way to rid yourself of body hair, but it starts to grow in the next day and can leave your skin feeling like sandpaper, which is why most women only resort to it in dire emergencies (last minute beach date).

For longer-lasting smooth legs and arms, *sukkar* or waxing is a much better option. If you don't like the idea of having to go to a salon to get it done, you can always have someone come to your house and clean you up in the privacy of your home. Lasting from three to four weeks, these methods are a good alternative to shaving and are relatively affordable. For something a little more permanent, there is laser hair removal, which takes up to six sessions to become effective. It's pretty pricey and can be painful, so much so that it may make your little pink razor look more and more attractive.

While it is totally expected that women be as smooth as seals at all times – this isn't Europe, after all – for men, it's a completely different story. What women go through to stay well-groomed can sometimes seem like a fulltime job,

and all a guy has to do is take a shower and wear deodorant and we're supposed to overlook the fact that he looks like he has a bear rug stapled to his chest and back.

Men don't seem to realize that hairy backs are just not sexy… at all… under any circumstances. It is not a sign of their virility, as many would like to think, but rather their lack of consideration towards the tastes of the fairer – and less hairy – sex.

Men tend to give the excuse that getting laser treatments or having their backs waxed is just not manly. Okay, but being mistaken for a furry animal at the beach is better? What's worse is the guy who wears a sleeveless tank with hair on the shoulders and back protruding from every area the material doesn't cover. If you're not going to remove the fuzz, at least cover it up! We don't need to see that – really, we don't.

So, how do you get your guy to get some grooming of his own? First, there's always blackmail – if he doesn't do this tiny little thing for you, then you can punish him in other ways (use your imagination, ladies!). You could also go a different route and tempt him into doing it by making him an offer he simply can't refuse – tit for tat, if you will. Or you could just hand him this book and tell him to take a look at this passage: Hey guys, if you're reading this, your lady wants you to wax your back already!

Chapter II
Prêt-à-Porter

Material girls

Fashion for Lebanese women is like what water is to plants – basically, they can't live without it. Although at times it may appear that many ladies here dress alike, Lebanese style is pretty versatile. One could probably group women into three main categories: the brand-obsessed, the go-betweens and, finally, the no-namers. Within these separate categories, there are a multitude of variations and subcategories, ranging from the conservative to the 'what do I need a bra for' crowd. The common denominator, however, is always fashion!

DESIGNER be thy name

Luxury names are an obsession that originated with fashion. From handbags to shoes, right down to undergarments, some women put all their pride and joy into their designer wardrobe… even if they can't afford it! The obvious fix for such addicts is buying fakes, some of which are so well done, no one is the wiser as to the real origin of the garment or accessory. Passing it off as an original is tacky, for sure, but what everyone else doesn't know won't hurt them!

Some women, however, go even further. They are so desperate for big name brands that they will go to great lengths to give the impression that they are designer madams through and through.

The truly obsessed go beyond buying fakes to **sewing designer labels** onto their discount brand items,

especially ones they are likely to remove, like a cardigan, so that when they take it off, the designer label appears in its full glory to all present. Just imagine, if these ladies put as much effort and innovation into actually earning a living, they could probably afford an unlimited supply of designer goods in their own right.

You can easily spot these types out and about because every piece of clothing they own displays a loud logo of some designer brand or the other. After all, what's the point of buying luxury if nobody knows you're wearing it?

In the MIDDLE

Women who fall under this category tend not to make it their life's ambition to sport solely luxury garments, but believe in owning three basic essentials for everyday wear: designer jeans, a designer handbag and designer sunglasses. These women are loath to wear fakes and would rather have a few original designer items than a closet full of imposters. Although they may think that it's always best to dress in designer duds from head to toe, they figure they can get away with wearing other regular brand names by mixing and matching with these main essentials.

These women easily stand out in a crowd, especially during sale times. When this ever important season is about to begin, you will see them clutching to their phones for dear life, waiting for that vital SMS announcing that their favorite boutique has started its sale.

If the 20% sale is still a little out of their budget, they patiently wait for the 50% and then, the highlight of their month, the 70% discount!

A jubilant expression when walking out of a store with a couple of shopping bags will be the first indication that you have just spotted one of the 'go-between' chicks!

The OUTSIDERS

The ladies of this fine category are not at all impressed with brand names and would just as soon walk on coals than spend more than $50 on a handbag or a pair of shoes. This is not to say that they don't care about the way they dress, but rather, they don't think that clothes have to cost as much as it would take to feed a small country to look good. They can be fashionistas in their own right without believing that a sense of style means having to wear screamingly giant designer logos across their chest or rear.

Not caring about luxury items not only frees their bank accounts, but also saves them from being slaves to fashion. And since they're not always competing with the brand-obsessed, they can focus their energy on more productive matters (like hair and makeup!).

Bare NECESSITIES

In Lebanon, to be considered even remotely 'fashionable' by the brand-obsessed or the go-betweens, you absolutely must own at least one designer bag. Men don't seem to understand the depth of a woman's obsession with her handbag, and words alone cannot explain the phenomenon here in Lebanon. No matter how spectacular your outfit is, if you don't top it off with a Prada, Chanel or Fendi, you might as well be wearing rags. Of course, it also helps if everything you pull out from inside said bag is also designer, like the wallet, sunglasses and, yes, even key chain.

When you've finally made the decision to become part of the stylish elite and splurge on one of these luxurious leathery delights (designer logos visible, if you please), be sure that you make the right choice. Don't even think of passing off your fake as an original to your friends – a fashion catastrophe almost as serious as not owning a single designer item – especially if they are even slightly fashion forward.

Anyone familiar with couture can sniff out a bogus bag faster than it will take you to blow your most recent paycheck.

To avoid being 'outed,' or duped into buying a fake for designer bucks, check out these helpful hints.

DON'T BUY THAT BAG IF:

- The guy selling it is called something like Abu Sami, who also sells fish of questionable freshness and imposter perfumes, all from the trunk of his beat up 1953 Mercedes.
- The so-called designer name is misspelled – e.g. it's Prada and Gucci, not Prala or Gussi.
- The colors or logo have clear smudge marks.
- The inner lining says 'Made in Taiwan.'
- The vendor tells you it's worth $500 but he'll give it to you for $50.
- The sales person takes you into a secret back room to show you the 'goods.'

Shoes, glorious SHOES!

Do you have a passion for Prada? Marvel at Manolo? Gush over Gucci? Go crazy for Cavalli? If you answered yes to any of the above, then you're not alone. In Lebanon, the devotion to flats, strappy sandals, pumps, boots and everything in between is probably the one unifying factor bringing women across the country together, regardless of their different backgrounds. Like all great love stories, it is a passion that has only grown more intense over time – and it doesn't seem likely to abate anytime soon.

The world's top scientists have desperately tried to discover what it is about shoes that drives women from all walks of life absolutely nuts – sadly, all have failed. Maybe it's the smell of the supple leather, the delicateness of the straps, the elegance of the heel…. Oh, who are we kidding? For the chic Lebanese, it's all about the name! But, if you can't always afford the pricey brands, it's okay, you don't need to move out of the country. Lebanese women are forgiving towards non-designer items in this fashion category, mainly because logos are not always printed on shoes, so you can't really tell who's wearing what! This means that you can get away with donning regular or discount brands as long as the styles are *à la mode*.

For your feet to fit in, you must pay close attention to fashion fads and follow them religiously. Keeping up with finicky trends is, therefore, a must. In general, in winter, you must own several boots in different colors and in the top styles of the season. In the summer, it's all about the open-toe sandal, so be sure to keep your feet in tiptop condition! This means regular pedicures every ten days to a maximum of three weeks (no skimping), exfoliating at least once a week, and putting cream on your feet everyday (nothing is uglier than a chafed heel – yuck!).

No matter the season, time of day or where they are, though, fashionable females are always on the lookout for a great pair of shoes – always.

Many a woman across Beirut will stop dead in her tracks if she spots a pair of beauties on someone else's feet. She will have no qualms about walking up to a complete stranger and exclaiming, *"Yiii, shoo mahdomee skarbeentik!"*

Which translates into: "Oh my, your shoes are so adorable!" And then the wearer of the shoes gets to say, with pride, "*Merci,* they're Dolce & Gabbana."

Yes, shoes just have a way of bringing women together. The fairer sex figured out a long time ago that it's shoes, not money or love, that make the world go around. Now, if only men could connect with their inner Carrie Bradshaw and bond over their footwear, maybe there'd be world peace!

A matter of STYLE

Style is most certainly a matter of taste, but when out and about in Lebanon, it seems that some women have decided that the less amount of clothes they wear, the sexier they look. So, to keep up this 'hot' persona, many girls at nightclubs or bars tend to wear the tightest of pants, and the skimpiest of tops (bra optional), while strutting around in the highest of heels. It's difficult to imagine what these women are thinking when they get dressed. Don't they realize that being sexy does not entail wearing two Band-Aids and some dental floss and calling it an outfit? Generally, a little more material is necessary (and in most cases, so are bras).

So, what is sexy? Not leaving much to the imagination most certainly is not. A little mystery is enticing and will get the guys wondering what else there is to you. But if everything is displayed before him in plain view on a silver platter, there isn't going to be much left for him to discover on his own. Most fashion experts agree that as a rule, if you're going to bare a little bit on top, keep yourself covered on the bottom, and vice versa. And, you don't need to announce to the world that you're wearing a thong by having it stick out from your pants or skirt. You're not going to get a prize or anything, so keep it *underneath* the clothes – they call it *under*wear for a reason! Now, that's not too complicated, is it?

The ultimate ACCESSORY

In Lebanon, everything is bigger, better and grander than everywhere else on the planet. This is no clearer than in the Lebanese woman's favorite accessory. Can you guess what the item could possibly be? Here's a hint: it's less alive than miniature couture puppies carried around in a Louis Vuitton bag, a lot shinier than Jimmy Choo shoes and smaller (in most cases) than a Porsche Cayenne. Have you figured it out yet? If you guessed diamonds, then take your bejeweled, manicured hand and give yourself a pat on the back because you are right!

The results may still be out on whether or not size does matter in other departments, but when it comes to these gems, the bigger, the better – no doubt. Marilyn wasn't kidding when she crooned that diamonds are a girl's best friend – she must've had a Lebanese soul! From wedding bands to drop earrings, sparkling stones are the surest and quickest way to the Lebanese woman's heart (are you paying attention, men?).

But, before you dart out to your favorite jeweler to pick out a big fat bauble for yourself, keep in mind that finding the perfect diamond is no easy feat.

There are actually **different grades of diamonds,** from the purest of the pure sparklers to the ones that make cubic zirconia look good.

To protect yourself from buying a dud, always keep in mind the Four C's – color, clarity, cut and carat – to help you separate the good from the gaudy.

On the diamond color scale, stones are graded from D to Z, the D to F range being the purest white and most coveted color. The darker the color, the lower the grade and value. For clarity, the scale starts with perfection at FI to flawed beyond measure at Imperfect (I3) as listed in the facing table.

The Gemological Institute of America (GIA) Grading Scale

CLASSIFICATION	MEANING
Flawless (Fl)	No inclusions or blemishes.
Internally Flawless (IF)	No inclusions and only minor blemishes barely visible under magnification.
Very Very Slightly Included (VVS1 & VVS2)	Minute inclusions barely visible under magnification.
Very Slightly Included (VS1)	Minor inclusions difficult to see under magnification.
Very Slightly Included (VS2)	Minor inclusions somewhat easy to see under magnification.
Slightly Included (SI1)	Noticeable inclusions easy to see under magnification.
Slightly Included (SI2)	Noticeable inclusions very easy to see under magnification
Imperfect (I1)	Obvious inclusions usually easy to spot with the naked eye.
Imperfect (I2)	Obvious inclusions easy to spot with the naked eye.
Imperfect (I3)	Obvious inclusions very easy to spot with the naked eye and which affect the stone's durability.

When it comes to the cut, contrary to popular belief, this does not refer to the shape of the stone – like the brilliant, princess, baguette, emerald, pear or oval – but rather the reflective and refractive qualities that constitute its brilliance and shine. So, if you really want to blind people with the dazzle of your sparkler, pick a cut that is not too shallow or deep. Last, but certainly not least, we come to the final 'C,' carat, or the weight of the diamond. This is probably one of those rare cases when being a little on the heavy side is actually considered a good thing!

One very important thing to remember, though, before you bring out the checkbook and cough up the big bucks, is to always ask for a certificate of authentication from a reputed institution – i.e. either from the GIA or the Antwerp High Council Institute of Gemology (HRD). Happy hunting, ladies!

Chapter III
Girls Just Wanna
Have Fun!

Party town!

No matter what cities around the world you've visited, the greatest party town of them all is undoubtedly Beirut. So, go ahead and put on your dancing shoes, ladies, it's time to party! Wait! Before you strap on those stilettos, be sure to go through the following essential steps below will ensure you smooth sailing when navigating the city's fabulous clubbing scene. Consider them the Six Simple Rules to enjoying Beirut's infamous nightlife to the fullest.

1. Crowd PLEASERS

First things first: pick the people you want to paint the town red with. Make sure it's a mix of guys and gals because an overdose of estrogen can be really boring for obvious reasons. Plus, guys can be particularly helpful when a venue is jam packed, especially when you have to visit the little girl's room and you literally need someone to shield you from aggressive shovers and people stepping all over your feet, as well as wayward drinks and cigarette butts. Other uses for males are that they make good dance partners (well, better than a girl at least), will usually drive so that you don't have to get home by yourself late at night and, if you're single, they can also make you look popular with the opposite sex when there are hot guys around. Do not assume, however, that your guy friends are always going to foot the bill – *très tacky!*

2. The VENUE

Although this seems like an easy enough step, in Lebanon, nothing could be more complicated than deciding where to go. You'd think there were a million choices to pick from making it all the harder, but that is not the case.

Beirut is the *only* place to go clubbing in the country and anyone who's anyone will either go to the Monot or Gemaizeh neighborhoods.

Both areas are swarming with the hippest and newest bars in town. True, it can be hard to keep up with what's in and what's not on any given week, but that doesn't excuse you from being seen in a joint even your grandmother wouldn't call cool. Even when you think the place has been settled on, there'll be at least one person in the group who doesn't want to go there, forcing you to start all over again. Some people spend the whole weekend deciding where to go and don't realize it until Monday morning, when they're back at the office wondering where Saturday and Sunday went. What's even more annoying is sitting in the car all night driving around Beirut, with no one able to make up their mind on where to have a drink. The highlight of your evening ends up being a *mankouche* (Lebanese sandwich) from Bliss Street that you eat in the backseat of your friend's car while listening to cheesy '80s music on the radio.

To avoid this from happening to you, always start planning your weekend on Monday. Pick a place, call up everyone and say that the decision has already been made, and don't give anyone a chance to suggest an alternative. Make it sound like it's a done deal – either they're in or out. No dillydallying, or you'll never get to go out! Sometimes, if you want a job done right, you have to do it yourself.

3. Yes, RESERVATIONS

There are always two scenarios for going out in Beirut:

1. Scenario one – no reservation

You and some friends couldn't be bothered to call in advance for a table, because like everyone else in Beirut, you decided to go out at the last minute. So what if it's Saturday night – if you go early enough, you'll probably be able to find a couple of spaces at the bar, right? WRONG! Unless, by early enough, you mean dawn, when last night's partiers are heading home, finally leaving their seats free. Once you get there, at about nine o'clock in the evening (only nobodies are seen out before then), the bar is already packed. Your friend wearing the low cut top manages to get the bartender's attention and order all your drinks. By ten, the place is crammed from wall to wall – you can barely breathe, let alone move. You're wishing you didn't have that second cocktail, because now you have to go to the bathroom and you're not sure you can make it back to your friends alive. You decide to stick it out and wait until you get back home. You've been standing for almost two hours now, feet aching in your heels, squished against some random guy, who you're pretty sure just rubbed up against you – and not by accident. The lack of oxygen starts to make you dizzy and to top it all off, the crazy dancing chick with no concept of personal space just dropped her drink all over your new shoes. Enjoyment factor (on a scale of one to 10): 0. 'I feel like a total loser' factor: 12.

II. Scenario two –
have a reservation

You've been friends with Ramzi a long time. He's a good guy, sure, but that's not why you keep him around. You see, Ramzi is the most connected guy in town – there's not a single bar owner that he's not friends with, making it a cinch for him to get a table anytime, anywhere. Every smart girl in Beirut makes sure that there's at least one Ramzi in her entourage, because going out without a reservation and being forced to stand up for hours on end is simply not a viable option. Once a place is chosen and the reservation is taken care of, all you have to do is show up and have a good time. You don't have to worry about the hostess with the clipboard standing outside the club rejecting people dumb enough to venture out on a Saturday night without a reservation. Just mentioning Ramzi's name gets you ushered right through the door to the safety of the table, where the party's already started. You have a seat, someone pours you a drink and then your favorite song comes on – and you and your friends dance until dawn. Once in a while, you look over at the pit of commoners standing near the bar trying to enjoy themselves while getting pushed around. You smile to yourself and think, 'Thank God I'm not one of them.' Enjoyment factor: 10. 'It' girl factor: 12.

So, what's the moral of the story?
Always - always - make a reservation.

4. Fashion STATEMENT

Choosing the right outfit to party in can be taxing, especially if you haven't been keeping track of who has seen you in what over the past few weeks. You never want to be seen in the same outfit twice – what, you want people to think you can't afford to buy new clothes? Low rise, tight, designer jeans are the staple going out attire, paired with a sexy top (avoid wardrobe malfunctions: wear a bra!). High heels are always a must, whether in boots or pumps. Most Lebanese women probably haven't worn flats when out since they were 12 years old. (For more tips on what and what not to wear, check out Chapter II!)

As for hair and makeup, girls can go over the top when going out, so try to keep things a little subdued. Whether up or down, your locks should always look perfect with not a strand out of place (see Chapter I for details). Your 'do should also last you the night – so keep in mind extenuating circumstances like dancing and humidity if it's summer and the venue is outside.

You don't want to walk in looking like a goddess and head home looking like a poodle!

When it comes to makeup, the typical Lebanese gal sure does like her dark eyeliner and mascara (pronounced *mass'ka'rah*). A lot of women also seem to think that no one is going to notice if they've gone over their natural lip line with lip liner. This will probably be hard to hear but, ladies, unless you're a real expert at applying makeup, exaggerated lip liner always shows. After a couple of drinks, the smudges around the mouth are not pretty, so unless you want to head to the bathroom to reapply after every sip, better stick to the pout you were born with.

4. A DRINK, please

Enjoying a lip-smacking cocktail while out clubbing is always fun. Overdoing it and getting plastered, however, is not. So, make sure that you keep to your limit (two to three drinks will usually suffice) so that you don't end the evening in the company of the toilet bowl. Also, if you're part of a group table, don't feel compelled to partake in the bottles of vodka that are usually requisites to getting a reservation. Feel free to go on your own and order a girlie cocktail. Often times, deciding on what drink to order can get complicated. So, to help you out a little, read through this list of popular cocktails and be prepared the next time you're out.

COCKTAIL	WHY IT'S GOOD
Amaretto Sour	For the ladies with a sweet tooth, this cocktail pairing the sugary almond taste of Amaretto with a sour mix is a great choice. Try it with a cola for a yummy cherry coke flavor.
Appletini	What James Bond would drink if he were a girl, this variation of the traditional martini contains either apple juice, apple cider or apple liqueur, vodka and a sweet and sour mix served in a martini glass, either shaken or stirred.
Blue Lagoon	This delicious blend of lemonade, vodka and Blue Curaçao is the same color as the deep blue sea, making it the perfect choice for a party at the beach!
Caipirinha	It's the national cocktail of Brazil, which could even rival Lebanon in the party to the extreme category, which is why this combination of sugar, lime and cachaça is just what the doctor ordered.
Chocolate Martini	Chocolate tastes good paired with anything, and that is especially true when it comes to this yummy drink, which combines vodka and crème de cacao.
Cosmopolitan	The quintessential girl's drink, this pinkish-red concoction is basically a mix of vodka, cranberry juice and triple sec served in a martini glass. It's stylish and tastes oh so good!
Frozen Daiquiri	Smooth, cool and divine, these cocktails come in many flavors and contain a tasty mix of rum and fruit juice over crushed ice.
Kir Royal	Usually served in a champagne glass, this is a marvelous cocktail made with blackcurrant liqueur and champagne.

COCKTAIL	WHY IT'S GOOD
Long Island Ice Tea	Don't be fooled by this cocktail's name – with, among other ingredients, a combination of gin, vodka, white rum and tequila, the only thing it has in common with iced tea is the color! So, if you're in the mood for something with an extra punch, this is your drink.
Mai Tai	It's rum, triple sec and lime juice served over crushed ice and topped with a maraschino cherry and sometimes even a slice of pineapple, so what's not to like?
Margarita	A tequila-based drink, the frozen variety is delightful and refreshing, especially in the hot summers. Usually served in a cocktail glass with a salted rim, you can choose from a multitude of flavors, but nothing beats the original lime.
Mojito	A tropical treat, this drink is a mix of rum, brown sugar, club soda and lime juice, topped with sprigs of mint.
Piña Colada	A rum-based drink with coconut cream and pineapple juice, there's even a song named after this delicious cocktail. You'll definitely be in the mood to party after a couple of these!
Seabreeze	A fruity mix of vodka, cranberry juice and grapefruit juice, this drink will certainly cool you off during those balmy Beirut nights. A final squeeze from a lemon wedge gives it that extra zing.
Tom Collins	A refreshing combination of gin and sweet and sour mix, it's like lemonade with a kick!
White Russian	If the weather is starting to remind you of Moscow, you might as well go with the flow and order this rich drink of vodka, Kahlua and cream over cubed ice. If you're in the mood for something darker, use cola instead of cream as a mixer to make it Black!

6. Dancing QUEEN

A good DJ is an essential part of any decent Beirut nightclub, because he or she is the one charged with electrifying the atmosphere and putting the crowd in dance mode. Sometimes, the awesome tunes are so loud you can feel the beat reverberating in your heart. When that happens, Madonna's voice usually creeps into your head, telling you to get up on the dance floor and move to the music. Of course, this being Lebanon, she also reminds you to strike a pose à la Vogue. If you're an exhibitionist and must jump on the table or bar top to strut your stuff, just be sure that you are not wearing a short skirt.

A nightclub, no matter how racy, is not a strip joint, so save the pole dancing for a more private and discreet occasion.

Whatever you do, don't make the mistake of spending the evening sitting down watching everyone else have a good time. You're lucky enough to live and party in Beirut, the greatest city on earth, so get up and let everyone appreciate the fabulousness that is you: one hot Lebanese woman! Just like Madonna said, you're a superstar, yes, that's what you are!

Chapter IV
Gimme a Break!

Relax, take it easy

Although Beirut is the party capital of the Middle East, sometimes a girl needs to take the night off to recoup her clubbing energy. Every now and then, you just get sick of the crowds and the smoke and the loud music and the people stepping on your feet and the drinks spilled on your shoes and creepy guys hitting on you and bitchy women staring you up and down and waiting ten hours for the valet to get your car. A weekend away from all the mayhem will give you the stamina you need to get back on the horse and return to *la vida loca à la Libanaise!*

No one said that a weekend at home has to be boring. If you want to be alone, there is nothing like curling up with a good book and your favorite chocolate bar. If you're looking for something good to read, when it comes to literature, the possibilities are endless, but below are a few suggestions.

GENRE	TITLE	WHY IT'S READABLE
Cheeky	*Life's Like That* – Michael Karam and Peter Grimsditch	A hilarious look at life in Lebanon with some great caricatures to brighten up your evening.
Cheeky	*Son of a Witch* – Gregory Maguire	A clever take on the life and times of the infamous Wicked Witch of the West from the beloved *Wizard of Oz* film.
Chick lit	*Lipstick Jungle* – Candace Bushnell	The witty exploits of three highly successful women at the top of their game. It's the same author that brought us *Sex and the City*, so you're bound to love it.
Chick lit	*The Devil Wears Prada* – Lauren Weisberger	Also a hit movie, this book tells the tale of Andrea Sachs, assistant to the devilish editor of a major fashion magazine. It's full of great humor and a little romance to boot!
Classic Romance	*Jane Eyre* – Charlotte Brontë	If the perfect novel existed, this would definitely be the one. It's the classic story of 'plain' governess Jane and her love, Mr. Rochester. You'll wish you were back in 19th century England!
Classic Romance	*Pride and Prejudice* – Jane Austen	This novel is the epitome of romance, following the love story between the ever-so-charming Elizabeth Bennet and the debonair Mr. Darcy.
Epic	*World Without End* – Ken Follett	A grand tale full of love, heartache, mystery and history. You will be so captivated by the main characters Caris and Merthin that the 1,000-plus pages will fly by. You should also read the prequel, *The Pillars of the Earth*.
Epic	*The Saxon Chronicles* – Bernard Cornwell	Mighty Saxon warrior, Uhtred, takes you on an unforgettable journey as England fights the Vikings. Start at the very beginning with the first book, *The Last Kingdom* – you will be hooked from the first sentence.

GENRE	TITLE	WHY IT'S READABLE
Fantasy	*The Harry Potter Books* – J. K. Rowling	If you don't know what these books are about, then you've probably been living under a rock for the past decade. The stories of boy wizard Harry and his pals as they battle the evil Voldemort are probably the most fun you'll ever have reading.
Fantasy	*The Lord of the Rings* – J.R.R. Tolkien	Follow Frodo Baggins as he tries to save Middle Earth in a truly tantalizing tale of another world, full of hobbits, dwarves and elves.
Mystery	*The Alienist* – Caleb Carr	An intense murder mystery set in 1896 New York City, the novel follows esteemed 'alienist' Dr. Lazlo Kreizler as he and his team try to catch a diabolical serial killer.
Mystery	*The Da Vinci Code* – Dan Brown	One of the most successful novels of all time, the plot revolves around a historic mystery that has been kept secret by a clandestine society for centuries – and it is up to famed symbologist Robert Langdon to crack the case.
Romance	*The Cider House Rules* – John Irving	The story of Homer Wells, who goes on an odyssey of sorts as he discovers life, love and himself.
Romance	*The Glass Lake* – Maeve Binchy	Romantic and witty, this story takes you to the Irish town of Lough Glass, where you will become immersed in the captivating lives of its charming residents.
Thriller	*Misery* – Stephen King	Paul Sheldon is a famous writer, who after getting in a car accident is rescued and imprisoned by psychotic nurse, Annie Wilkes. Be sure to check out the movie when you're done with the book!
Thriller	*Primal Fear* – William Diehl	When a popular archbishop in Chicago is murdered, it's up to brilliant attorney Martin Vail to defend the accused, Aaron Stampler, and uncover the shocking truth behind the crime.

If you're in the mood for some company, you could always have a couple of girlfriends over for a movie night to watch your favorite chick flick.

Forget about your hair and makeup and what outfit to wear, just slip on your favorite tracksuit (Couture, as in Juicy) and you're ready!

If you're in a jam about what to watch, read across for some of the most popular chick flicks – and what snack foods go best with each film!

YOU'RE IN THE MOOD FOR...	CHICK FLICK	WHY IT'S GREAT	THE SNACK FOOD
Period Romance: as in, wistful and dreamy	*Pride and Prejudice* (or any other Jane Austen film – including *Sense and Sensibility* and *Emma*)	Elizabeth Bennet frolics in the beautiful English countryside and falls madly in love with the dashing Mr. Darcy. It's as far from Lebanese reality as there is, but what else are dreams made of?	Hot mugs of English tea with scones and jam and assorted mini cakes from your favorite bakery.
Period Romance: as in, some day my prince will come	*Ever After*	What girl doesn't like a good Cinderella story? It's the happily ever after ending that we all want – plus the prince is really hot.	A slice (or two) of your favorite cake or pie with either hot chocolate or decaf coffee.
Romantic Comedy: as in, it could happen to you	*You've Got Mail*	It's the internet age, so it's entirely possible that you could meet Mr. Right online – and he just may be really, really cute and really, really rich and think that you really, really look like Meg Ryan!	Practical snacks, like fat-free frozen yogurt and sugar-free chocolate with unsweetened ice-tea or lemonade.
Romantic Comedy: as in, you can relate to this story	*Bridget Jones's Diary*	Inspired by *Pride and Prejudice*, Bridget Jones is a 30-something, overweight, working woman who drinks too much and smokes too much, but manages to find love nevertheless while having a raucously good time.	Do it à la Bridget and bring on the booze. Mix your own margaritas or daiquiris (but leave out the cigarettes) and order a pizza or two, plus dessert of course!
Teen Romance: as in, nostalgic for high school	*Clueless*	It's loosely based on Jane Austen's *Emma*, so what's not to like about this hilarious teeny bopper flick revolving around Beverly Hills über chick, Cher, and her quest for love?	Everything that reminds you of being young: soft drinks, ice cream and cookie dough (or kill two birds with one stone with cookie dough ice cream).

YOU'RE IN THE MOOD FOR...	CHICK FLICK	WHY IT'S GREAT	THE SNACK FOOD
Teen Romance: as in, where was he when I was growing up?	*Say Anything*	Worth watching just for the scene when hopelessly smitten Lloyd tries to win back his lady love, Diane, by standing outside her bedroom window holding up a portable stereo blasting Peter Gabriel's classic love song, 'In Your Eyes.' Oh, sigh.	A movie so sweet that you're better off sticking to the salty stuff, like potato chips, nachos and Doritos.
Action: as in, anything guys can do, girls can do better	*Alien*	The first female action star, Sigourney Weaver kicks alien butt as Ripley, a member of a rescue crew sent to a strange planet crawling with creatures that have an appetite for humans!	Get the real cinema feel by turning out the lights and making movie-style popcorn with an ice cold soft drink.
Action: as in, who needs men?	*Thelma and Louise*	Gun slinging best friends Thelma and Louise dump their men, run from the law and cause havoc in this ultimate road trip adventure. Still not convinced? Umm, Brad Pitt with no clothes on – need we say more?	Go for something a little more hardcore, like a bottle of red wine and dark chocolate. You won't need much else – did we mention, Brad Pitt, no clothes on?
Classic: as in, they don't make them like that anymore	*Casablanca*	If you're in the mood for a golden oldie, this is the movie to watch. You'll hear some of the most famous movie lines of all time – like, 'Here's looking at you kid,' and, 'I think this is the beginning of a beautiful friendship.'	Since it takes place in Morocco, try some Arab delicacies with Turkish coffee, of course.
Classic: as in, irresistible epic love story	*Doctor Zhivago*	Who can resist this tragic tale of Lara and Yuri (Omar Sharif at his best)? A classic so beautifully romantic, you'll wish you were born in Soviet Russia!	Since it takes place in the freezing Soviet Union, prepare steaming cups of hot chocolate with marshmallow bits with your cookies of choice and some Rice Krispy treats.

If you're not in the mood for a movie, you could try hosting a theme night: anything from your favorite board games to a wine and cheese tasting, or maybe even a combination of both. Inviting a few friends over to the house will keep you from getting lonely, while also giving you a break from the clubbing scene. At the same time, you get to put on your best Martha Stewart imitation and show off your hostess skills.

For something a little original but low-key and easy to pull off, try throwing a wine and chocolate soirée: with chocolate as the main star, it's sure to be a hit and the preparation is minimal!

CHOCOLATE	WINE
Either semi-sweet or sweet dark chocolate	A full-bodied Zinfandel or Cabernet Sauvignon.
Strawberries dipped in dark, sweet chocolate	A white Zinfandel, because it has a hint of strawberry flavor.
White chocolate	Semi-dry white wine with a burnt aroma and hint of sweetness, or a semi-dry sparkling wine work best.
Chocolate cheesecake	Try a non-oak Merlot.
Chocolate mousse	Pinot Noir red wine (slightly chill it first).
Milk chocolate	Sweet wines with flavors of dried fruit, spices and oak (you could also pair these with dark chocolate sweets).
Bittersweet chocolate	A full-bodied Cabernet Sauvignon – it has a slight bitterness with a roasted earthy flavor, which you could also use in any sauce for a bittersweet dessert.
Bittersweet chocolate cake (with a raspberry sauce)	Go for a young red wine.

Source: Paul Koder, Wine Consultant, Wine Trend, Inc.

Morning and afternoon DELIGHT

If you prefer to keep your evening free, then you always have the option of hosting a get-together earlier on in the day. Your best bet is the *subhiyeh*, a traditional Lebanese event that every Lebanese woman should experience at least once in her lifetime – where else is a girl supposed to learn the fine intricacies of the art of gossip? Taking place in the morning, which is where the name comes from, the typical *subhiyeh* requires minimal preparation: a big bowl of *tabbouleh*, a tray of *mu'ajinat* (savory pastries) ordered from a local bakery, an array of desserts of your choice (either homemade or ordered) and, of course, the all-important Turkish coffee.

Western women may occupy their days with soap operas, but in Lebanon, women get all the drama they need from the juicy tidbits readily supplied at any given *subhiyeh* – and the more scandalous the information, the better.

It should come as no surprise that whenever a bunch of Lebanese women are gathered together in one area at any given time, the main course is always gossip!

Also on the activity menu is coffee cup reading *(tubseer)*. No true *subhiyeh* would be complete without having your future told through the patterns left in your coffee cup! To make your *subhiyeh* complete, be sure to invite at least one woman who claims to have the gift of foresight (the always popular *bassara*).

In general, if you're single, be prepared to hear news of an *arees* (prospective husband), who's on his way to you but is held back by some undistinguishable obstacle. You will probably hear such tell-tale helpful details like he is male, you may or may not know him, he may be fair or dark, tall or short, live in Lebanon or abroad, etc. As to why you're not married yet, the cup will undoubtedly reveal that the *a'yn*, or evil eye, is the culprit, because

if you have the dreadful luck of still being single, then you surely must be cursed.

For married women, your life's most coveted ambition – finding a husband, of course – has already been accomplished, so there's not much else in your future except for a phone call or letter from abroad with – wait for it – news! Imagine that. As for the career-driven, it is perplexing why you would want to hear about anything other than romance, so the cup is unlikely to highlight any future developments that have nothing to do with getting yourself a husband.

When the coffee and cup reading are over, it'll be time to bid your friends adieu. After a morning chock-full of *subhiyeh* chatter, you will most probably be looking forward to some quiet time in the evening, giving you ample time to digest the chitchat and soothsaying over some leftover dessert.

Chapter V
Calling All Friends

A friend indeed

In a television interview, celebrity heiress Paris Hilton once said that she recognizes a true friend by purposely wearing a hideous outfit and asking the person in question whether or not she looks cute. If the answer is affirmative, she knows she's got a rotten apple in her entourage. Most other women, however, probably don't apply such stringent measures when it comes to picking out the fakes. But, every person does have a certain instinct when distinguishing a genuine friend from the rest of the lot.

The old Latin adage goes, 'A friend in need is a friend indeed.' Much lauded as the truest expression of friendship, you would be hard-pressed to find a better description. Following this time-trusted proverb, the best way to figure out who is the truest of the true is to think of all the times you really needed a friend and remember who was really there for you.

Tests of true friendship can take many different forms – it's not like there's a checklist that you can just cross off. You could realize what a great friend you have when thinking of the time you really needed a job and she went out of her way to get you an interview at a great company without you having had to ask. Or the time you were stranded at a nightclub in the middle of the night and she came to pick you up and take you home, no questions asked. There are so many different ways of being a good friend, but all basically abide by the same concept: being there when needed.

Many times, women lose sight of what an asset a best friend can be, especially when marriage and children seem to take over their lives.

But, do not ever doubt that every woman should have at least one best friend. Who else are you going to call at all hours for a good gossip session?

Who are you going to complain to about that nasty witch at work who said you look fat in your new outfit? No one will give you a sympathetic ear like your best girlfriend.

You need someone in your life who just gets you, even when you're PMSing and going through Dr. Jekyll/Ms. Hyde mood swings. You also need someone to confide in and make you feel better when you've had a lousy day. Just be sure it's someone you can trust and who's been there for you in the past. Use your own judgment when deciding who is worthy of that ever-precious label 'best friend,' and don't bestow it too liberally. You never know, it could be as simple as having someone look you straight in the eye and say point blank: 'You look hideous in that outfit.'

A little time with YOUR FRIENDS

You should always make the effort to get together with your girlfriends at least once a week, no matter how busy you think you are. There are so many great ways to spend time with your gal pals, and the good news is, you can do them at all hours of the day! So, don't waste another minute – leave all the men and other cumbersome stuff at home and get to it!

1. Schedule a weekly morning coffee session, or *subhiyeh,* so that you can gab over the week's events.

2. Get your manicures and pedicures or hair done together.

3. Treat yourselves to a day at the spa!

4. Go to the movies and catch the latest chick flick that your husband or boyfriend said they'd rather have their fingernails pulled than sit through.

5. Go shopping (like that even needed to be on a list!).

6. Take an art or language class together.

7. Start a reading group.

8. Become gym or ski buddies!

9. Double date with your significant others.

10. GIRLS NIGHT OUT! No explanation needed.

How to get through the SEASON OF THE WITCH

No matter how careful you are about choosing your friends, sometimes associating with someone you don't like is just plain unavoidable. She could be someone at work or someone who's married into your family – in short, cutting her out of your life is just not an option, however unfortunate that may be. It's the type of relationship where you know she doesn't like you and she knows that you don't like her, but because of the circumstances, you have no choice but to pretend that you both go together like a wink and a smile. (Well, there's probably a lot of winking and smiling going on, but not the friendly type!)

How many times have you found yourself in the company of someone that you have to be civil to when deep inside you're desperate to bitch slap her?

In fact, the very sight of her makes you wish you stayed home and had a carpet fluff picking competition with your cat instead. In such situations, when you know you're going to face a barrage of snippy comments, be prepared to stay cool, calm and collected – never give her the satisfaction of knowing that she got to you. It's never pleasant having to deal with people that you constantly have to be on guard with, especially those women whose only pastime seems to be coming up with one-line zingers aimed right at you. The best revenge? Ignoring them with a wink and a smile!

If, however, you've had just about enough of the almighty *latshee* (zinger), and have way too often been too stunned into silence to come up with a comeback, only to think of the perfect response hours later, then perhaps it's time to take a different approach. Try practicing some of the comebacks to some of the most common rude comments below so that the next time you come face-to-face with a viper, you know exactly how to give it right back to her!

RUDE COMMENT	WHAT YOU WISH YOU COULD SAY	THE COMEBACK
Akbalik! Hurry up and get married before it's too late and nobody wants you anymore.	It's time to move out of the trailer park, hillbilly girl.	*Akbal* (may) you do something with your life that goes beyond getting married and having kids.
Wow, you've put on so much weight. But it looks good on you.	[Take the heaviest object nearest you and whack her on the head with it.]	Yes, *hamdillah*, unlike most people, I have the kind of face that can take a few extra pounds.
Have you ever considered liposuction?	See above!	No? Have you?
Haven't you worn that dress before?	You call that hideous rag you're wearing an outfit?	My goodness, you must have a lot of time on your hands to take notes on what everyone is wearing.
What have you done with your hair?	It's called a haircut, you may want to look into getting one.	Just thought I'd try something new. A little style never hurt anyone.
Oh, you're not fat, you just have to lose weight on your thighs/butt (etc.).	Yeah, like you're Heidi Klum!	It's not about the weight, it's how you carry it.

The GRAPEVINE

Everyone gossips. Even if you think you don't gossip, you gossip. When you're sitting with your friends, drinking coffee, and you're talking about the night before when you were all in Gemaizeh and you bring up that girl with that outfit and that hair, you're gossiping. When you're in the office and having lunch with your colleagues and you start talking about how the boss berated the guy in accounting for coming in late, you're gossiping. When you're at the gym working out with your trainer and he starts telling you how many members come for the sightseeing rather than the exercise, and you ask him to point those people out, you're gossiping.

Curiosity may have killed the cat, but in Lebanon, it gets you an extra cup of coffee and a hell of a story to boot.

There's no sense in feeling guilty about it, it's only natural that you'd want to know who's doing what, why and where. In fact, gossip only becomes a real problem when it's about you. Neighborhood gossips are particularly bothersome, especially when the scandal of the century is when you come home in the evenings on the weekends and you're dropped off by – heaven forbid – a boy.

It doesn't seem like gossip is going anywhere anytime soon. It has become part of the patchwork of Lebanese genteel society – and that's a good thing. How else would we know what's happening with the Joneses? Let's face it, without gossip, our *subhiyehs* and daily phone chats with our nearest and dearest would be reduced to talking about the weather – and there's not much a girl can do to make that colorful. Gossiping about sexy plotlines from the latest soap operas, or the goings on of the hottest celebrities, may tide you over in a dry spell, but nothing will ever replace the real life scandals that could be happening among people you actually know in person!

In fact, nothing is more riveting than that juicy morsel, that tasty tidbit, that tantalizing bit of information that you're just dying to share so that you can watch the expression on your friends' faces, see their jaws drop and hear them exclaim, 'No way!' Afterwards, you can just sit back, cross your arms, nod knowingly, and think, *my work here is done.*

Fun vs. MEAN GOSSIP

The general rule about gossip is, as long as it doesn't hurt anybody, then anything goes. Anything that could seriously harm the reputation of someone or get them in trouble is definitely off limits. Just remember that your goal is to have a laugh and a good time, not to offend anyone, because how can that be entertaining?

Also, a distinction should be made between **friendly gossip between friends (fun)** and spreading rumors indiscriminately among everyone you meet (mean).

For more of an idea about fun vs. mean gossip, take a look at the table below.

FUN (BETWEEN CLOSE FRIENDS)	MEAN (TO ANYONE AND EVERYONE)
Remarking on someone's questionable dress sense or style.	Spitefully remarking that she can only afford to shop discount.
Laughing about how wild she was the night before at the pub.	Exaggerating her behavior in a way that would harm her reputation.
Making fun of what she said when someone asked her a serious question and she didn't know the answer.	Filming the incident with your phone and posting it on YouTube.
Speculating on what was eating at her the last time you saw her.	Making up possible scandalous scenarios between her and her significant other.
Joking about a random chat conversation you had with her.	Saving the chat conversation and sending it to other people.
Remarking how an outfit she was wearing was really unbecoming to her figure.	Happily talking about how fat she's become.

The ENTERTAINER

Sometimes, the prospect of having to entertain for consecutive days on end can be incredibly stressful, especially if you're having guests from abroad come and stay with you. The thought constantly on your mind is, 'What am I going to do with them all day long?' But the Lebanese did not get their famous reputation for hospitality by handing their guests a guide book, putting them in a *service* and saying, 'See ya later.'

Lebanese hospitality is a time-old tradition that is passed down from generation to generation. Most visitors are truly impressed with the warmth and generosity of their hosts, which is why, today, we have a lot to live up to. Before you fret over composing the perfect jam-packed schedule for your out-of-town friends, just remember that Lebanon is full of fabulous sites and activities. The summer is an especially great time to receive guests. Other than famous sightseeing spots (see next page for details), the obvious first destination is the beach! From Beirut and Batroun to Jiyeh and Tripoli, the golden shores of Lebanon are a delightful way to spend an entire day. By renting a boat, you can go sightseeing along the coast and stop over at one of the famous ports – such as Sidon or Byblos – and have a great meal at a seaside restaurant.

The summertime is also festival season, so be sure to check out the programs at Baalbeck, Beiteddine and Tyre. You could even check out the sites during the day, and then enjoy a concert in the great outdoors in the evening. On the topic of the great outdoors, if nature and adventure is your calling, Lebanon is also an interesting place for ecotourism. Believe it or not, rock climbing, hiking, cycling and white water rafting are all activities a lot of people consider fun!

One of the most important attractions of Lebanon, though, is the food, so *numero uno* on your to-do list should be a traditional Lebanese lunch. Begin with the *mezzah* (appetizers); to entertain yourself, order really time-honored fare, like brain, tongues and testicles, and watch the shocked expression of your foreign friends as you explain what the dish is in a perfectly calm voice, as if it were as normal as eating a burger and fries. Foreigners are usually impressed with a fully laden Lebanese table and even discovering a bowl of *tabbouleh* can seem like they've found the Holy Grail. Another nice touch is the *nargileh* (traditional smoking pipe), which is the ultimate accompaniment to the perfect Lebanese meal.

Another great Lebanese tradition is wine, and what better way to explore the elixir of Bacchus than in the Bekaa Valley? Take a day to drive out to any of the vineyards and enjoy a scrumptious meal with some great Lebanese wine against the backdrop of the beautiful greenery. Some wineries are even open during the winter, with an indoor restaurant and, if you're lucky, a cozy fire.

With food taken care of, it's on to the next essential activity to do while in Lebanon: shopping. There's no better way for a girl to spend the day than spending money – and if your guest has the foresight to recognize the great importance of shopping, then it's time to hit the malls together. Don't forget to check out the great shopping districts of Verdun, Kaslik and Downtown. For winter vacationers, we mustn't forget the thrills of skiing down the slopes in Faraya and Faqra.

For the less sporty inclined, there's always the lure of hot chocolate in front of a roaring fire (add some marshmallows for anyone who needs extra convincing). But, whether winter or summer, Lebanon definitely has a lot to offer. By the end of your friend's trip, you'll be thinking, there's so much left to do and so little time to do it all. Save the ideas for the next visitor!

TOP TEN SIGHTSEEING MUSTS IN LEBANON

1. **Baalbeck** – Discover the wondrous Roman temples and then have a delicious meal in Zahlé.
2. **Beiteddine** – A beautiful old castle in the Chouf mountains, it's also a great spot to take in the awesome scenery.
3. **The Cedars** – Take a hike up the mountains and enjoy being surrounded by Lebanon's national tree.
4. **Downtown Beirut** – Restaurants, shopping and ancient Roman ruins – what more could you ask for?
5. **Jeita Grotto** – An ecological delight, a day at these caves is definitely an adventure.
6. **The National Museum** – The archeological marvels of Lebanon are truly a must-see.
7. **Sidon** – Visit the ancient Crusader fortress as well as the old souk and then end your day with a delicious seafood meal at the famous Resthouse restaurant.
8. **Tripoli** – A bustling city in the north, this town is perfect for sightseeing and has some of the most famous Lebanese pastry shops in the country.
9. **Tyre** – Beautiful beaches and a multitude of eateries offering tasty meals make this city worth a stopover.
10. **Zouk Mikael** – A charming old souk full of hidden treasures and a choice of great restaurants.

Chapter VI
The Ties that Bind

Bond, family bond

Most people consider the average family to consist of parents and a couple of siblings, but in Lebanon a family can make up an entire village, literally, what with all the aunts, uncles, cousins and grandparents, etc. Coming from a large family certainly has its advantages and disadvantages, but most Lebanese women would admit that without their many relatives, they would probably be the loneliest creatures on the planet. One of the reasons Lebanese families are so large is because everyone is still pretty connected to their roots, which makes it easier to keep track of various family members. Plus, to be considered 'family' doesn't really require much – sometimes the same last name is all you need to be called 'cousin,' even though there is no direct blood link.

Of course, having so many relatives means that you are bound to be stuck with a few that you don't particularly like so much – with any luck, they're the ones that don't live here – which could make things a little awkward when you meet up at certain events. Family squabbles are, in fact, pretty common and you are most likely to have one uncle, aunt or cousin who doesn't speak to the rest of the clan for one reason or the other (like the catastrophic time Uncle X did not call Aunty Y when her daughter got an 'A' on her fifth grade math final).

Also running rampant among most Lebanese families is competition. Your parents have bragging rights to you no matter what, so things start to heat up when you're young and they start showing off with your grades, awards you've won or how young you were when you graduated high school and college.

When you've moved into the job market, the competition moves on to your position, promotions you've received and what car you bought for yourself (bragging openly about how much money you make is too crass, so your vehicle choice gets the message across more subtly).

As a female, the 'who gets married first' race begins once you hit puberty and is especially heated between mothers, who are more than eager to get their daughters hitched at as young an age as possible. After you've tied the knot, the cycle begins again, but this time with your kids. And so, it is a never-ending, inescapable drama that keeps the family dynamic moving from generation to generation!

Despite the minor pitfalls of extensive family life, there are also many joys. Once in a while, you will find that nothing is more enjoyable than a big family lunch, with everyone sitting around the table eating *labneh* and *zeytoun* (yogurt and olives) – maybe there's a little gossiping going on, even a little competition, but in general, everyone has a grand old time. Yes, the family unit in Lebanon can be a wonderful thing, from *jiddo* (grandpa) right down to your mother's uncle's cousin's wife's sister-in-law's second cousin three times removed.

All in the FAMILY

You usually find one of these in every Lebanese family!

THE TYPE	HOW TO RECOGNIZE THEM
The Patriarch	Usually the grandfather, he's the boss and everyone knows it and competes to be in his good graces. He keeps the peace and makes sure everyone in the family is kept in line. His judgment is final and no one, no matter how old, will go against him – he is the judge and jury on all family disputes. Just call him Don *Jiddo*!
The Matriarch	*Sitto*, *teta* or just plain old grandma, she's the one who keeps the family together, organizing lunches and dinners and reminding everyone about birthdays and other milestones. She's a lot tougher than she looks – where do you think *jiddo* gets his orders from?
The Grudge Holder	He or she keeps a list of every time you failed to fulfill a family obligation and is sure to rub it in your face every time you see him or her. Unable to let things go, their favorite thing in life is to '*e'atab*' (hold a grudge).
The Gossip	Usually a female, she likes to think of herself as the family historian, rather than the family gossip. Her favorite pastime is to keep track of what everyone else is doing and then break the news to whoever will listen. She will use whatever means necessary to get the dirt, even an intricate network of housekeepers to make sure that every household is covered!
The Suck-up (a.k.a. the Saint)	The most annoying person in every family, he or she lives to show up everyone else by being the first to carry out a family obligation – and they will carry out every single one. They also expect to be the first in the family to be informed of important events, and they trumpet the fact that they were the first to know as a badge of honor.
The Black Sheep	The person who always comes in last in heated family competitions in the major categories of school grades, job title and marriage. They are least likely to show up at family functions because they are sick and tired of being constantly compared to everyone else.
The Overachiever	Their main goal is to outshine everyone else in terms of achievement. It starts at an early age with school grades and then moves on to occupation. It's not really about the money as much as the title. Accolades are also important, so that they can be framed and hung around the house or office, as are photographs with famous people. They feel they deserve more respect than others and any small infraction could injure their ego and incur their wrath for eternity!
The Success Story	The one who made it to the top! This family member has the fanciest house and cars and is always throwing big bashes at his or her place. They are very eager to dole out advice on how to make it big, even if you don't ask for it. They also like to brag about what great deals they got on pretty much everything they've bought. No matter what you're in the market for, they claim they could've found you the exact same thing, only for much cheaper.

Much OBLIGED

Lebanese families are usually tight-knit, and for the Lebanese woman this translates into an end-less amount of *wajbat* (obligations). Keeping up with the sheer multitude of relatives in your life and their various goings on – including birthdays, marriages, births, etc. – can be at times a lot of fun and at others, a big nightmare! The more you keep up with family milestones, the more the family expects from you, so that if you miss one, no matter how minor – Aunty Foufou left the city to summer in the mountains and you didn't call to say bye, making you the world's worst niece – you'll never hear the end of it.

If you're not careful, family *wajbat* will start to take up all your free time, so that *teta's* luncheons will be the highlight of your social calendar.

The trick is to get the clan used to you doing the bare minimum at an early age, so that when you actually do go out of your way to fulfill a family obligation, they'll be so grateful, you'll look like a

hero rather than a black sheep. This means not calling or visiting every aunt, uncle or cousin to commemorate birthdays, graduations, job promotions, getting good grades on a report card, getting a new car, having a haircut, buying a new pair of underwear, etc.

There are certain times, however, when you are compelled to partake in the family happenings, no matter how you feel about it. In this neck of the woods, nothing brings a family together like a *farah* (happy affair) and it is the general rule of thumb that any feuds among squabbling relatives be put aside if such an occasion arises. You may be fed up of attending engagements, weddings and congratulating your kin on their new bundles of joy, but basically there is no getting out of them. As a woman, if you skip out on one of these affairs, everyone will just think you're jealous, especially if you're single.

So, even if your cousin is marrying a guy who looks like he could be a descendant of Frankenstein - i.e. you're not envious in the least, but you just don't like her - you still have to put on your happy face and pretend to enjoy the festivities.

Then there are family visits, which are especially abundant during the summer when relatives living abroad arrive by the truckload. In such cases, it is customary that you go *'salmee aleyoun'* (say hello upon their arrival) and *'wad'iyoun'* (bid them farewell when they are about to leave). These visits usually include a lot of watermelon and Turkish coffee, with at least one relative or the other trying to explain how you are related by going through the family tree person by person starting from 1853.

Walking the fine line of maintaining good family relations without being drawn into every single family function can be kind of tricky. Keeping up with the family is a way of life here, so just be sure to attend at least one or two functions a year (one a season will do), especially on major holidays. You may never be crowned the queen of *wajbat*, but that's one title you could probably live without!

Nobody does it LIKE TETA

Grandmothers just seem to know how to cure everyday ailments with a simple herb and, surprisingly, a lot of them seem to work. Here are some of the most common Lebanese home remedies passed down from *teta* over generations.

AILMENT	REMEDY
Acidity and indigestion	*Laban* (yogurt)
Bad breath	Chew parsley
Colds	Floral herbal tea
Colds and stomach aches	Sage
Diarrhea	Sumac (sprinkle on boiled potatoes)
Dizziness and fainting spells	Rose water
High cholesterol	Flax seeds
Indigestion	Boiled cardamon
Sore throat and cough	Ginger (boil in tea)
Stomach aches	Boiled mint

Chapter VII
Looking for Mr. Right

Right place, right time

For single women, when it comes to meeting the perfect guy, most people will tell you that it's all up to *al nasseeb* (fate). But, unfortunately, there is no *nasseeb* market with a 'single men' aisle. If only it were as easy as going shopping and having all the available men lined up according to certain specifications – attention all shoppers: tall, dark and handsome doctors, aisle one; blue-eyed knights in shining armor, aisle four. Alas, such a world doesn't exist and *nasseeb* is not an almighty genie that will magically drop your own personal prince charming right onto your lap. So, if you want to meet your soul mate, you're going to have to do a little legwork yourself.

In Lebanon, your options for meeting single men are pretty limited. In the past, the only way for singles to meet was through families, whereby the *arees*, or prospective suitor, would visit a girl with his parents at her home in the presence of her parents. He may have seen her himself at some function or other and asked who she was, or have been told about her by family members without ever laying eyes on her. If after the visit the guy decided he liked the girl, he would ask for permission to see her again, provided, of course, the girl agreed. Sounds completely romantic, don't you think?

Thankfully, things have changed monumentally and the concept of dating has become commonly accepted by the average modern Lebanese woman. The problem now is where to actually meet prospective dates. In places like the United States or Europe, popular spots for singles to mingle usually include the workplace, gym, bus stops, laundromats and supermarkets. In Lebanon, though, those kinds of places are not exactly hotbeds of social interaction.

Although many single Lebanese women do work, most of the eligible men have left the country for better opportunities and pay abroad.

So, unless you're gay or looking for old married men, the workplace may not be the right place to find a date.

The same could be said of the gym, although if there are any single males left in the country under the age of 40 and above 22, you're more likely to meet them at the gym than any place else. Bus stops are also out of the question, because – ewwww – who wants to date a guy that needs to take public transportation? Although single males in Lebanon are a rarity, a gal still has to maintain her standards. Next on the list are laundromats, which don't exist here, and even if they did, you would never find an eligible Lebanese bachelor doing his own laundry. As for supermarkets, although they are aplenty, most singles, male and female, still live at home, so they are unlikely to do their own grocery shopping.

So, what does that leave you with? Although Beirut is undoubtedly a great place to party, one of the worst places to meet men is at a nightclub or bar. First of all, the music is so loud, it's not like you can have a decent conversation through all the noise. Second, guys out clubbing are usually looking for a fast hookup, not a wife! One of the best ways to meet people is through friends, so be sure to go out a lot with different groups. You never know who has a brother or cousin or friend who could be the man of your dreams.

Opportune times to meet young men are usually during the holidays, because that's when they all come back from abroad to visit family and friends.

The rest of the year could pose a bit of a dry spell. The best holidays are the short, concentrated ones, like *Eid al Fitr, Eid al Adha* or Christmas, because you know huge groups will all be coming at the same time. The summer is second best, but not really prime guy scouting time since it gives a lot of leeway for people to book their stay. Basically, your prince charming could come anytime between June and September, which makes it a lot harder to find him!

During any vacation time, be sure to get out more. If a friend or relative is going out with friends and invites you along, GO! Meet as many new people as you can, even if it's just a coffee or a trip to the mall. Remember, you meet people through people. So, even if you're introduced to a guy who brings new meaning to short, fat and bald, always consider that he may be able to introduce you to someone that will make you swoon.

Also, keep in mind that the wise elders weren't kidding when they said you'd have to kiss a lot of frogs before you find your prince. But, throughout the disappointments – and there will be many – always keep positive and you will find him… eventually. In the end, though, when you do meet Mr. Perfect (*inshallah*), be sure that *nasseeb* will get all the credit!

The FIRST DATE

Location. location. location

Picking out a spot for a first date can be tricky. It's usually up to the guy to choose a place and take care of the reservations. It's completely off-putting when date night comes along and he's totally unprepared and asks, 'So, what do you want to do?' Obviously, if he didn't care enough to plan a nice evening ahead of time, you shouldn't bother giving him a second date. If, however, prior to the date he asks what you'd like to do, that shows that he is considerate and thoughtful of your preferences, so it is perfectly acceptable for you to make a suggestion.

A great first date venue is a casual café, of which there are an abundance in Lebanon. Don't suggest a self-service place, because that could present an awkward moment when it comes to paying, especially if you're meeting there and one person arrives before the other. A casual café setting will put you both at ease and make for easy, pleasant conversation so that you can get to know each other.

A café in a mall is always a good idea because a) if the date is going well, it's an easy transition to doing something else, like seeing a movie or going to the bookstore, and b) if it's not going well, all the shops and crowds will make it easy for you to lose him fast!

If your date has skipped the casual coffee stage and already made plans for a lunch or dinner, be prepared. Such occasions are very important because they give you insight into male eating behavior – which can be a huge turnoff if his table manners are akin to a wild beast gnawing on its prey! If, for some reason, he doesn't seem to know that a napkin goes on the lap and that talking with his mouth full is just plain gross, you'll know that he's not date number two material.

As for you, try and order food that's not too messy – e.g. stay away from the spaghetti. You don't want food all over your face or clothes, giving the impression that you need a bib. You also don't want to be self-conscious that your mouth looks like a food disposal unit every time you talk or smile, so stay away from killers like parsley in *tabbouleh* or anything with *zaatar* (thyme). Another absolute no-no is any food with garlic or onions – no explanation needed for this one, ladies, it's basic bad breath etiquette 101!

For the first date with the guy that you're really not that into, or don't really want to go out with but have to because of extenuating circumstances, go see a movie. The conversation will obviously be kept to a minimum because you'll be busy watching the film, so you don't have to worry about talking to the guy. Plus, if you're really not attracted to him, there's the added benefit of not actually having to look at him. Be sure that you pick the film though, and stay away from anything remotely romantic. Your safest bet is the latest action/adventure flick – that way there's no risk of having to discuss intricate plotlines afterwards.

You've got the look

When it comes to the dress code for a first date, the most important thing to remember is that first impressions are everything. Just like you'll judge the way he parts his hair and whether the color of his socks matches his shoes,

> be sure he'll be sizing up your ensemble and whether or not you bought it from Hooker Outfitters.

Keep the 'girls' stowed away on a first date and dress casually, so that you don't look like you're trying too hard. Of course, you don't want to go to the other extreme and look like you're auditioning for the role of Maria in *The Sound of Music*. The happy medium is always best. It goes without saying that the perfect outfit also depends on the venue, so find out beforehand where he's taking you. If it's a casual coffee date, a nice pair of jeans and top will do perfectly. For dinner, if the restaurant is fancy, don't over do it, but choose something that is casually chic. Black always works best because you can dress it up or down. Best friends or sisters are a great help in these situations because they will honestly tell you whether your outfit works or not, so be sure to enlist the opinion of at least one person you trust to tell you the truth.

Word play

Conversations during a first date can certainly be awkward, especially if the guy goes on and on about how successful he is and what kind of car he's just bought (unfortunately, a common trait among Lebanese men). Impressing you with material items just shows that he doesn't have much else to offer. Some women may be into that, especially those that see a mate as someone who can merely provide unlimited manicures, pedicures, hair appointments, designer outfits and luxury cars, etc. For those looking for a little more substance, though, such flagrant self-promotion is about as attractive as a male baboon thumping on his chest for the attention of the nearest female – i.e. not at all.

Similarly, if he tries to overpower you with his so-called 'intellect' by bringing up hot topics like politics and religion and then bashing you if you disagree with his 'profound insights,' you'll know that the guy is simply not for you. Such heated debates are definitely not first date conversation material. Topics should be neutral and aimed at getting to know a little more about the background of the person, not whether he supports one politician or the other. If such a subject comes up, don't bother engaging in the debate, just try and change the subject, or let him rant while smiling and nodding; don't order dessert and get out of there as fast as possible.

Here are some tips on what topics you should bring up during a first date and those you should stay away from.

ACCEPTABLE	UNACCEPTABLE
Brief accounts of your background – e.g. university and where you grew up.	Listing all your academic accolades, or describing all the horrors of your childhood.
Saying what you do in life to show that you have future goals and ambitions.	Boasting about how successful you are and how you just spent $1,700 on the latest Marc Jacobs bag.
Talking about your hobbies and interests so that you don't seem boring.	Letting him know how often you get a bikini wax.
Making light jokes about yourself to highlight that you have a sense of humor.	Being self-deprecating to the point that you wouldn't even date yourself.
Talking a little about your friends so he knows that you're popular and well-liked.	Treating your date like he's Dr. Phil and going into detail about past failed relationships and trashing your ex.
Casually bringing up your family to point out that you have values.	Going on as if marriage between the two of you is a done deal and start talking about what your kids will look like.
Asking neutral questions about his life and background while showing interest in his answers.	Making him feel like he's part of the Spanish Inquisition and aggressively probing about personal and intimate details.

LOVE ME don't

Getting out of accepting a date with a guy without hurting his feelings, but making sure he gets the message and doesn't call again, can get complicated. You could try going with something completely obvious, like the time-old cliché, 'I'm washing my hair,' which would definitely let him know that you don't want to go out with him. But, whatever you do, don't be a complete coward and not pick up on his calls.

Unless he's a **total horror story** - in which case he deserves the worst treatment - try and get out of it with a little finesse so that you come out looking like a class act rather than... well, **a bitch**.

Here are some good tips on getting out of a date. Be sure to end each excuse by saying that you will call him. When you don't call, he'll understand.

- You're not feeling well (e.g. having stomach cramps)… but will call when you're feeling better.

- You have an important family function that you can't get out of… but you'll call when you're free.

- An important work thing came up and you're really busy at the moment… but you'll call when you have some free time.

- You're going up to your family's mountain village to visit relatives for the weekend… but you'll call when you can.

- Company suddenly came over and you can't leave the house… but you'll call him when you can go out.

The previous are not exactly nice ways of letting a guy down, because you know you're not going to call, but at least they're gentle. Of course, you can always take the brave route and tell the guy the truth: 'I really enjoyed meeting you, but I don't think this is going to work out and I'd rather we just remain friends.' Guys may hate to hear the 'friends' word, but sometimes the truth hurts!

Going in BLIND

No matter what anyone says, any gal who's gone through it will tell you that there's nothing worse than a blind date. How many times have you heard that someone wants you to meet a guy who's great, handsome, charming, smart and successful only to find that he's a toad with the manners of an ape and the intellectual capacity of a *mankouche*? There's no point in sugar coating it: Blind dates are just not fun. Sometimes you're lucky and meet nice people, even if they're not of any romantic interest, but those cases are few and far between.

Unfortunately, most Lebanese are obsessed with marriage – parents are obsessed with marrying their kids off, and singles are equally occupied with finding lifelong mates. In certain situations, being single and of a marriageable age in Lebanon is incredibly stressful for women, who are harassed by family members for the simple fact that they haven't yet agreed to settle down. Single women face countless criticisms for this seemingly disastrous state of affairs – accused of being too picky, too snobby, thinking too much of themselves, etc. – everyone has their own theory on why you are not married, but it doesn't matter, because inevitably, it's always your fault. For this reason, many women are often pressured or bullied into accepting blind dates, even against their better judgment – 'Why don't you want to meet him? He's a doctor!' God forbid you even ask what he looks like – so what if he has more hair on his back than his head, as long as he's the same religion and comes from a good family, what's not to like? Yes, how incredibly superficial of you to worry about genetics and the possibility that your children could turn out to look like gremlins. No matter what questions you ask about the guy, you're always told to 'just meet him and find out for yourself.' What they don't seem to understand is that finding out such information beforehand is extremely important because

there is no point in spending a
millisecond with someone when,
even if he were
the last man on earth,
you'd rather inject yourself with the same
virus that wiped out the rest of
the planet than be in his company.
Oh, the rough travails of the
single Lebanese woman
- *ya haram* (poor things)!

Instead of explaining why blind dates don't work for you, sometimes it's just easier to bite the bullet and do it. In such cases, it's always a good idea to have a contingency plan for an easy escape. First, always have a friend call exactly 30 minutes into a date, which gives you the chance to give some excuse that will allow you to ditch him immediately. Another good idea is to meet during a lunch break, because then you know that you're only stuck for a maximum of one hour.

During the date, don't act like a total diva, even if you don't like the guy. Lebanon is a small country and you don't want to get the reputation of always turning men down (because then, horror of all horrors, you'll never get married). Be civil and polite, but don't ask a lot of questions about him so that he gets the hint that you're not that interested. Answer his questions pleasantly, but don't go into detail. At the end of the date, shake his hand courteously and say that it was nice meeting him (thank him if he paid). If he's in the country for a visit, tell him you hope he enjoys the rest of his stay (he'll get the hint that you don't want to see him again). If he suggests another date, say that you will call him.

If you actually like the guy and want to see him again, then congratulations, call the *Guinness Book of World Records* because you're one of the rare few who actually got set up with a decent guy! Hey, stranger things have happened!

Should he stay or SHOULD HE GO?

Here are some telltale signs of whether the guy you're out with is in to you or if you should drop him faster than last year's accessory du jour. Conversely, if you want a guy to know that you're interested in him, look out for the signs in the left column!

HE'S INTO YOU IF...	LOSE HIM IF...
He looks at you admiringly.	He continuously stares at your chest.
He strokes his hair – he finds you attractive.	He keeps scoping out the room, obviously checking out other women.
He nods while you talk – he's interested in what you're saying.	He keeps looking at his watch when the topic turns to you.
He strokes his leg – subconsciously, he wants you to touch him.	He rearranges himself in front you.
He licks his lips – he wants to kiss you.	He pounces on you without warning and shoves his tongue down your throat, causing you to gag.
He rubs his neck – there's definite sexual attraction.	He suggests getting a room for the night.
He insists on paying, even though you offer to pay for yourself – he's generous.	He splits the bill, showing that he has the worst quality of all: stinginess!

The Ex-Factor

Getting over an ex is never easy. Just as *nasseeb* can be credited with finding love, it is also equally used as the perfect little scapegoat for all relationships that don't work out. So, if you just don't feel like talking about why one of your relationships ended, just say, '*Ma kan fee naseeb,*' it just wasn't meant to be.

The first thing to remember is that it's okay to be upset over a breakup – it does not mean that you're pathetic or emotionally weak. Your feelings are not a tap that you can simply turn off and on (if only it were that simple!). It's okay to talk about your heartache with those you trust, but don't make it the main topic of all your conversations. It's good to get things off your chest, but some things you just have to deal with on your own. Your friends are there for you, but you should not consume them with your problems – they have lives and troubles of their own. You should also prepare yourself to accept their advice, even if they say things you don't want to hear.

Sometimes, when you're getting over a guy, it's difficult to remember that the world doesn't revolve around your present unhappy situation. Your close friends and family will understand this and be patient during your grieving period. However, you need to help yourself too and not dwell on the past. Getting involved with work and other activities – keeping busy and occupied – will help take your mind off things.

This would a great time to join a gym – take out your anger and frustration on the treadmill! Some girls prefer wallowing in a tub of ice cream, but it's always better to take the looking fabulous rather than fat route. Another form of therapy is shopping, but don't abuse your credit card – it didn't break your heart! Pretty soon, you'll be thinking about him less and less – the (well-deserved) degrading nicknames you and your friends penned for him will lose their luster, and in no time at all, you'll be able to say his name and even see him again without so much as a flinch. Just be sure to do one thing: go out with your girlfriends a lot and remind yourself that

there is no greater place to be unattached than in Beirut, where friends are fantastic, the nightlife is notorious,

the fashion is fabulous... and where the single are still sensational!

THROUGH THICK AND THIN

To help a friend get over a relationship, try these simple tips:

- Let her know that you are always there to listen, but don't let her continuously monopolize conversations with stories of her ex.

- Sympathize with her situation and show that you can relate.

- Be firm with your advice – don't let her do something you think will set her back.

- Take her out a lot.

- Don't ever say, 'Snap out of it!'

- Don't encourage her to jump into a relationship right away.

- Take her with you on shopping trips or to the movies.

- Avoid bringing up how great your own relationship is, if you're in one.

- Stop her from comparing every guy she meets to her ex.

- When she's ready, encourage her to give other guys a chance.

Chapter VIII
Here Comes the Bride

The Wedding planner

The typical Lebanese wedding is a huge affair – sometimes even bigger. Since most women here start planning their big day at age seven (maybe even younger), it should come as no surprise that when the moment arrives, it is the single most important day of her life. The pressure for every Lebanese woman to get married before she hits 30 is intense, which is why mothers, future mother-in-laws, aunts and grandmothers are equally at fault for making weddings into outrageous spectacles. The competition factor also pushes families into making their daughter's wedding into a grand extravaganza that out-shines, out-costs and out-dazzles every other previous bash.

So, even after a girl has overcome the obstacle of actually finding a husband, she is pressured into planning the party of all parties. The smart gal will bypass all the hassle and hire a wedding planner – an investment worth every penny. He or she will take care of rounding up your options in just about every category, so all you have to do is pick which you like best. That way, you can check off the venue, menu, flowers, entertainment, invitations, wedding registry, chocolate and souvenirs from your to-do list with a minimal amount of stress.

The wedding planner can't help you out when it comes to picking the perfect dress, though, which is totally up to you. Wedding gowns can either be store bought – prêt-à-porter style – or specially made for you by a designer. The cost of a brand new gown, however, can be heart-stoppingly expensive, which is why many a young bride has opted to rent her bridal wear.

The sentimental types may not mind coughing up upwards of thousands of dollars for an item of clothing they will only wear once in their lives, but some may decide that using the money to buy useful items, like say, furniture, is more important.

Another area where the wedding planner won't be much help in is putting together the guest list. Do not underestimate the hardship associated with this arduous task – made all the more difficult by large families. Unfortunately, most relatives, even the ones you don't like, have to be included to avoid serious feuds, which is why aunts, uncles and cousins end up making 90% of your wedding party. You should also be prepared for relatives insisting that their spouse's uncle's wife's cousin eight times removed be invited along with his significant other and brood of seven children.

After the guest list has been drawn up, it's time to set up the seating arrangement – also known as, 'this is what hell must be like.' No matter how much time and effort you put into the seating chart, there are always going to be people complaining about where you placed them – also known as, 'dealing with massive Lebanese egos.' One aunt or uncle will undoubtedly fume over being seated so far from the dance floor, or too close to the kitchen, or with people not important enough. You're not going to be able to please everyone, but to avoid a fiasco, try dividing the venue into different sections, with several tables in each, giving people the chance to sit with whomever they please in their allotted area.

As for the photographer, why not kill two birds with one stone and get one of the social magazines to cover your swanky event? You never know, you may even land on the cover! Not only will you get professional snapshots to keep in your very own album, but the rest of the country will get to admire your sophisticated party taste and see how to really throw a wedding. Once all the nitty-gritty has been taken care of, you can focus your attention on the fun part: the party!

Let's CELEBRATE!

It's here – it's finally here! It's your big day and you're about to become a Mrs. *Wu akheeran* (finally). In most Lebanese weddings, religious ceremonies are usuallly held before the evening celebration and, unless taking place in church, are usually private affairs with only close family members present. This means that the nighttime affair is solely reserved for your amusement and that of your guests – so get ready to party like a rock star, which should be relatively easy since Lebanese wedding bashes are notoriously extravagant.

The typical wedding celebration begins between 8pm and 9pm and kicks off with a brief cocktail session of about half an hour – brief being the operative word since nearly every female guest will be wearing heels and forcing them to stand for longer than that is just pure torture. When the mingling is over, it's time to head to the dining hall, where, hopefully, there will be no major outbursts resulting from the seating arrangement.

An hour after that, the bride and groom will usually make their grand entrance, complete with a musical serenade and dance troupe in traditional Arab dress, more commonly known as the *zaffet aroos*.

Some couples go all out with their walk down the aisle, with accompaniments of fireworks, fog machines, falling confetti and other such fanfare. The *zaffee* is undoubtedly the highlight of the whole evening, and sometimes a party is wholly judged based on the grandeur (or lack there of) of the bride's entrance.

Once the happy couple has arrived on the scene, they will almost immediately open the buffet, or the waiters will start serving the meal if it's a seated dinner. Sometime after that, they will have their first dance, which can also include special effects similar to a cheesy music video on Melody Hits. Speaking of cheesy, the dance is usually followed by either speeches, or a slide show or video montage showing old pictures and footage of the bride and groom long before they were Mr. and Mrs., with a sentimental pop song playing in the background.

At a successful wedding celebration, the above usually transpires pretty swiftly to avoid boring guests into a coma. And, when it's all over, the party really begins! At an average wedding, entertainment is pretty much limited to a DJ, a live band, or both.

Some couples like to go all out and hire big name acts to entertain their guests, but the smart bride knows that she should be the star attraction of her glorious night, not some Miss McBigBoobs entertainer.

Plus, you don't need to spend oodles of money on a celebrity when all it takes for a wedding to be loads of fun is a friendly bride and groom who make sure that all their guests are on the dance floor and taking part in the celebration.

At about midnight, it'll be time to cut the cake – also a big production. The trend nowadays is to use a giant fake cake with an equally giant-like sword to saw through it. Waiters will then swirl around with mini-cakes or slices on plates that are placed on each table. This is usually the cue for the champagne, which should be kept flowing freely to ensure that every guest gives your wedding rave reviews the next day.

Before you walk down the aisle, make sure you've covered all your bases by going through the list below.

WHAT TO DO FOR YOUR BIG TO-DO

- **Buy comfortable shoes** – Most brides make the mistake of buying ritzy heels that they can barely walk in, let alone stand and dance in for hours. Don't fall into this trap and get shoes that won't kill your feet.

- **Venue** – If you're getting hitched in the summer, remember the heat and humidity before you choose an outdoor setting. Never underestimate the importance of air conditioning.

- **Lighting** – A lot of brides never even think about lighting, but with an indoor setting, lights set the ambiance and transform the ballroom from red carpeted, tacky dining hall to snazzy party central!

- **Entrance** – Be sure not to make your grand entrance too late in the evening, because your guests will get bored and may leave early.

- **Hosting** – Every bride should remember that she is also hosting a huge event, so be sure to go to every table and thank your guests for coming and take pictures. It's also very important to dance a lot and get the guests involved if you don't want them to go all Cinderella on you and leave at midnight.

- **Speeches & movie** – You may want to screen any speeches that will be made to ensure that no one is going to bring up any embarrassing revelations from your past. Sometimes, the bride and groom will decide on a video made by their siblings or closest friends instead of a speech, so be equally cautious that the footage is suitable for all audiences.

Madame TROUSSEAU

Other than planning for all the celebratory fanfare, brides have to prepare their trousseau, or *jheiz*, to make sure they have everything they need to make a smooth transition to wifehood. What does this entail? In the days of yore, most of the trousseau was handmade by mothers, grandmothers or aunts, and the more opulent the garments and accessories, the more affluent the bride was considered. Today, things are a little different – mostly thanks to the delightful invention of the mall – and preparing the marriage chest has become just another excuse for the bride to do a whole lot of shopping! Are there no downsides to getting married? Well, don't forget about dealing with the in-laws!

As most couples receive oodles of gifts and even cash from the wedding registry, the modern trousseau is usually all about the bride and doesn't contain a lot of items for their new home. For tips on what a traditional marriage chest with a contemporary twist usually contains, read below.

- **Cedar chest** – To store all the goodies before you start cohabitating with your significant other.

- **Lingerie** – No explanation necessary (one should hope not, at least!).

- **New wardrobe** – You really can't expect to wear the same clothes you wore when single.

- **Jewelry** – As if a brand-spanking-new dazzling diamond solitaire, accompanying diamond band and wedding band were enough. Not even!

- **Linens** – You really want to trust a guy to pick out your bedroom set or formal tablecloths?

- **Bath towels** – See above.

- **Toiletries** – There is no way around it: your husband is going to see what you look like without makeup when you get up in the morning. But, you still need your beauty tools for the rest of the day.

- **New luggage** – Get ready for your honeymoon and any other sexy trips you plan to take with your hubby with a matching set.

SEXY time!

Otherwise known as the honeymoon, for many Lebanese couples, this is probably the first time they will go on holiday together. There is no need to go into detail about what you should be doing during this intimate time, but here are some things to consider when planning your romantic getaway.

IF YOU CHOOSE...	BE PREPARED FOR...
A beach destination	Bad hair days. Every bride wants to look fabulous during her honeymoon (for the pictures that will later be posted on Facebook), so bring along a hairdryer.
An exotic locale	Food poisoning. Third world countries are fascinating tourist spots, but their restaurants are not generally known for hygienic practices. In case you forget to avoid anything uncooked or to stick with bottled water, bring along medicine for upset stomachs and other such ailments.
A cruise	Sea sickness. Take the right medication so that you don't spend your honeymoon in bed – and not the fun way!
Somewhere cold	Bulky clothes. Thick winter clothes may be a little difficult to fit in a suitcase, but don't worry if you forget the gloves or scarves – just think of all the fun you'll have snuggling with your honey for warmth!

'Akbalik' and other things you shouldn't say to your single friends

When your time has come to tie the knot, don't forget about the single friends that were there for you long before your soon-to-be hubby came along. The first thing to remember is that even though your wedding is definitely huge – to you – and exciting – to you – and wonderful – to you – your friends may not give it that same degree of importance. This does not mean that they're jealous or not happy for you, but just that they have other things going on in their own lives and don't fully understand what the big deal is since it hasn't happened to them yet.

Try and be sensitive towards your single friends and don't rub it in their faces every five seconds that they're being left behind as you embark on a new and better chapter in your life. If you alienate your buddies during this special time, you will regret it later when the honeymoon is over, you're not the center of attention anymore and things have settled back to normal. You will most likely find yourself lonely and missing them terribly. To make sure this doesn't happen, keep your gal pals involved with the planning of your big day – ask for their opinion and advice and try to assign them certain tasks so that they feel like a part of the happy occasion rather than mere spectators.

MOMMY and me

After you've tied the knot, the next logical step is, usually, having children. One of the greatest joys for any woman is motherhood, and for the typical Lebanese female, like everything else in her life, even having kids is a designer affair. From couture outfits to designer diaper bags and deluxe baby carriages, the shopping possibilities for your tots are endless. Your child, after all, is an extension of you and your fashion sense, so be sure that you always complement each other in the wardrobe and accessory departments.

One aspect of baby care that most Lebanese moms cannot live without, though, is the housekeeper/nanny - how else is any self-respecting woman supposed to raise her children?

The modern Lebanese family would, in fact, be incomplete without this integral member of the household. On any given weekend, you will be hard pressed to find any child unaccompanied by the hired help, whether at a restaurant, the mall or even the beach. Wherever you see a Lebanese kid, be sure that his or her nanny is not far behind supervising the child's every move during what is supposedly 'family time.' (During such family outings, every parent should keep in mind that although screaming tots running around public places may be adorable to you, others might consider such actions a little on the annoying side. It's true that every child is the apple of their mother's eye, but don't expect everyone else to feel the same way about your kid.)

Another must when having a baby in Lebanon is to pick out a unique name. Gone are the days when a simple Lebanese moniker would do – if you want your child to have any sort of social life at the sandbox, you'd better hit the drawing board to come up with something that doesn't sound even remotely Arab. For some help on picking out the perfect name, you could try surfing the internet or buying a book on baby names. When it comes to making your final choice, remember that all things French are, naturally, more than acceptable, and if you pick a name that isn't, make sure that it can be pronounced with a French accent.

Of course, there is a lot more to having a baby – from breast pumps to baby monitors and picking the right pre-schools – but the superficial basics are a must before you even consider reproducing. With all the above down pat, you'll be ready to rear your spawn in style, and really, what more could a new mommy possibly hope for?

Chapter IX
Working Girl

It's a hard knock life

In Lebanon, there are three main reasons why women work: 1) They love what they do; 2) They need the money; 3) They're single, bored and need something to keep them occupied until they find a husband. No matter what category you fall under, one thing's for sure, the rapid depletion of males – young and old – from the country means that offices in Lebanon are overflowing with estrogen. The collection of so many women in one space may be every guy's dream, but for the average gal, it can feel like she's joining the bitch brigade rather than the workforce.

When women are grouped together, you see, they tend to get pretty competitive with each other, which can make the work environment, at times, a little on the unfriendly side. But, one advantage of having a majority of females at the office is the abundance of gossip on-hand. Naturally, the downside is that at any given moment, the women could turn the tables on you and talk about the way you styled your hair that morning and how those pants make your butt look big. Not very sexy news, for sure, but with barely any men in the office to spice things up – i.e. naughty office romances – the gossip department could hardly be expected to be any juicier.

Although the opportunities for love at the workplace are pretty slim and the gossip can get catty, the real careerist won't even notice. She's there to make her mark on the world, and getting ahead through hard work is her ultimate goal, not the husband hunt. It's easy to spot the lady with the serious work ethic, as she always arrives to the office on time, declines to partake in office gossip (for the most part) and does not whine when she has to work overtime to meet a deadline. She's also on hand off-hours in case an office emergency comes up and is willing to work on holidays if need be (shocking, but true).

For the employed woman who cares about her job as much as the fundamental inner workings of a vacuum cleaner, she will pretty much do the opposite of the above.

Since getting a pay check and whiling the hours away until walking down the aisle are her main priorities, this lady's workday is kept to trying to look busy while accomplishing little to zero. Her main strategy at the office is to constantly complain about how diligently she slaves away and how tired she is to mask the fact that she actually does nothing at all. It's an art form perfected by these dames of disinterest, who are so adept at feigning hard work, sometimes they even fool themselves.

careerists vs. BRIDES-IN-WAITING

If you're not sure what kind of working girl you are, answer the questions below to find out.

1. Is your resume of excuses for being late to work longer than your actual work resume?

2. Do your bathroom breaks last for over half an hour?

3. Are your work meetings in actuality giant gossip fests?

4. Do you take a day off work every month for cramps?

5. Do you consider your job as merely free access to the internet?

6. Is the word 'deadline' missing from your vocabulary?

7. Will you quit the moment you get a marriage proposal?

8. Does your workday schedule look anything like the following?

   9am-9.30am: Arrive at the office.

   9.30-10am: Make morning coffee and chat with the gals about anything but work.

   10am-11am: Call up friends while pretending to talk to clients and make important work contacts.

   11am-1pm: Check email, Facebook and chat online while pretending to write up reports.

   1pm-3.30pm: Lunch!

   3.30-4.30 pm: Play solitaire while pretending to do research.

   4.30-4.45pm: Do actual work.

   4.45pm-5pm: Start packing up to leave.

If you answered 'yes' to any of the questions, then you are probably not a careerist! Having a rewarding job and being a successful member of the workforce is certainly not one of your main ambitions in life, so you're going to have wait patiently for Mr. Right to come along. Don't worry, he'll get here… eventually (hey, it's Lebanon – he's probably stuck in traffic!).

Excuses, EXCUSES

Sometimes, even if you're serious about your job, getting to the office on time can be a problem. Of course, there are also those who simply can't be bothered to roll out of bed to face another day pursuing a profession they hate. Whatever the reason, if you're finding that punctuality is getting the better of you, take a look at some of these excuses for being tardy that should be able to get you out of a jam. Just be sure not to use clichés, like traffic (you should've left the house earlier), or your car broke down (why didn't you take a cab?), or your alarm didn't go off (get a new alarm), as they are now completely ineffective due to overexploitation!

1. The electricity went off and your garage door wouldn't open, or you got stuck in the elevator.

2. You had an allergy attack and couldn't come in until it eased up.

3. The bank called and there was an emergency with one of your accounts that had to be taken care of immediately.

4. Anything to do with a child, if you have one.

5. Your filling fell out and you had to get to the dentist right away.

6. They're doing construction in front of your home and a big truck was blocking your car.

To make your excuses believable, try to call the receptionist on your way to the office to let her know that you're running late because of any of the reasons above. That way, if your boss asks about you, he or she will know that you phoned in, making you seem more responsible, plus it saves you from having to give him or her the excuse directly, which could be more intimidating.

If, on the other hand, your boss has a sense of humor and you don't make it a habit of coming in late, you could turn your tardiness into a joke by saying you got lost, or were having a bad hair day. The head honcho may appreciate your wit so early in the morning and give you a break.

Women AT WORK

If you thought deciding what shoes to wear with your new outfit was tough, just think about having to make the possibly life-altering decision of what career path to follow. Daunting, indeed! With so many professions, specialties and sub-specialties to choose from, it's a wonder that more people don't make a full-time job out of picking a full-time job. To make things a little easier for you, read about some of the job options available for women in Lebanon and what personality types are best suited for them.

THINK ABOUT...	IF YOU ARE...
Advertising	Creative, sociable and a good team player, with thick enough skin that you won't crumble if and when a client or boss doesn't like your ideas.
Banking or finance	Good with numbers and are okay with strict work hours, including a half day on Saturday.
Business	Experienced, ambitious, a leader and have the means and capability of managing finances as well as a staff.
Cosmetology	More comfortable with a makeup bag than a designer one and able to transform an ugly step-sister into Cinderella with lipstick, eyeliner and mascara.
Engineering (architectural, computer, civil and even mechanical)	A whiz at math, like to build things and are more than happy to be the only female in an otherwise all-boys club.
Fashion	Always on top of fashion trends, in love with clothes and accessories and believe that you were the editor-in-chief of *Vogue* in another life.
Graphic design	Artistic, creative and comfortable working on a Mac.
Interior design	Stylish, innovative, have great taste and a way with fabrics, colors and furniture so that you can easily create beauty in just about any space.
Journalism	Good at writing and/or editing and willing to work erratic hours, including holidays, to meet deadlines. If interested in reporting, you must also have what it takes to get your story, no matter how tough.

THINK ABOUT...	IF YOU ARE...
Marketing	Sharp, tough, a leader with strong analytical skills and the discipline to consistently stay tuned to changing trends.
Medicine	Great at biology, able to stand the sight of blood without puking, are not squeamish about cutting up cadavers and have an innate need to help the sick.
Public Relations	Outgoing, personable and have creative ideas as well as super organizational skills.
Sales	Friendly, persuasive and rarely take 'no' for an answer, with the ability to make moss growing on a log sound alluring.
Teaching	Patient, good with children and are okay with never being able to strike it rich unless you win the lottery or marry a millionaire.

SETTING UP shop

Are you rich and looking for something to do that doesn't require working like a slave for mere pennies? If yes, then why not do what like-minded Lebanese women in the same situation are doing and open up a shop? Don't worry, no prior experience or knowledge of business is necessary – all you need is a rich daddy willing to cough up the capital for your little venture. Then you can go and rent or buy a space in a swanky neighborhood, put up a sign with a chichi name and call it your own business! Sounds easy enough, right?

The most popular business
for such young ladies seems to be a boutique, usually stocked with so-so items sold for
quadruple their value.

If this is a move you're contemplating, a good idea is to get several girlfriends (i.e. their daddies) to go in on the venture with you as 'partners.' All you have to do after that is hire a couple of sales clerks to run the store and you can just pop in once in a while to see how everything is doing and pick up the profits (if there are any).

Advertising and marketing are not usually one of the main concerns of this contemporary Lebanese businesswoman, as most of her client base consists of her entourage of friends. These buddies will will come to the shop to show their support and, although the prices will be exorbitant, they'll go ahead and purchase an item or two (no one wants the reputation of being a cheapskate).

Although some privileged young ladies may take this easy route to doing something with their lives, other Lebanese women actually do have the gumption and talent to open up a business on their own and make it work without any outside help. These types usually stock their boutiques with their own creations, or travel extensively to find the hottest trends and kudos go to them for their independent, hardworking spirit!

BANKING for dummies

Now that you're making your own money, it's time to get acquainted with your finances, which can be a little more complicated than receiving a monthly allowance from mom and dad. The first thing to do is open a bank account. It's a good idea to open two accounts – a checking (for shopping sprees) and a savings (for future shopping sprees). You collect interest on the latter, so be sure to pump it up every month so that the amount increases over time.

When it comes to the checking account, think of it as 'fun money,' as this is the sum you set aside for personal expenses. Decide how much you need a month to keep up the lifestyle to which you've become accustomed and put the rest away for a rainy day (in the account that generates interest). Once you decide how much money you can play with each month, it's a lot more fun spending it, because you know you can afford the stuff you're buying and can leave the guilt behind.

Opening your own account also means you get your own debit and credit cards. Debit cards are basically automated checkbooks without the bulk. It operates like a credit card except that the amount is immediately withdrawn from your account after it has been swiped. The downside of these babies is that the ease of use makes it difficult to keep tabs on how much you're spending. Before you know it, you could wipe out your entire bank account and not even realize it until your phone bill comes in and you don't have enough money to pay it. It's a lot more embarrassing to get a call from your bank saying that your account is overdrawn than having to turn down that new designer handbag – so wipe away those tears and go ahead and put it back on the shelf (at least, until you can afford it)!

The credit card, however, much like the name suggests, operates on credit. Each card has a limit depending on your credit history and how much money you have in the bank, which means that you can spend up to that amount every month. But, before you rush off to buy that yacht, keep in mind that you have to pay the money back! Each month, you have to cough up a percentage of the total amount you owe, with the outstanding sum collecting interest, which you have to eventually pay off as well. Yikes! The worst thing for your finances is living in debt, so,

before you crown your credit card
your BFF (best friend forever) remember
that you should never live
beyond your means, no matter
how sparkly that diamond in the window is!

Chapter X
Big Bytes

timedia café

Your inner geek

Getting in sync with technology today is about as necessary as breathing and drinking water. If you don't have an internet hookup then you've probably been living under the proverbial rock for the past few decades. Today, absolutely everything is dependent on the greatest invention of the 20th century, the World Wide Web. How did we ever survive without it? Do you even remember the days when there was no Google or Hotmail? Or when you actually had to write letters or school papers by hand (or even worse, with a typewriter)? How about going to work and not having a computer screen in front you, but having to – imagine the horror – actually do stuff by hand?

Those were the days, technophobes might say. But, for the rest of the computer-loving folks out there, being without a computer is probably akin to losing a limb (of course, to the average Lebanese woman, the same could be said about cell phones, see ahead for details). Every modern Lebanese should have a home computer – how else is a self-respecting woman supposed to keep in touch with friends? Otherwise, you might as well get a tattoo reading 'cavewoman' on your forehead, because that's how all your friends are going to view you.

As with everything in this country, even your computer is an issue of fashion. The model, make and size all reflect your rank in the ever-finicky Lebanese society. Today, you have your choice of PCs, laptops and even all the features of your computer in the palm of your hand, thanks to the multitude of handheld PDAs.

Even if you don't exactly need a computer, you still absolutely must own one.

Nothing spells social suicide clearer than being spotted at – of all places! – an internet café (unless, of course, you are only there for the coffee, which is perfectly acceptable). One distinction should be made, however, and that is if you bring your own laptop to a café with a wireless hotspot. This is not only acceptable, but in fact encouraged, as it is prime opportunity to show off your fabulous techno-accessory!

The best way to decide what personal computer you should buy is to research the different brands, taking into consideration your requirements – including memory, price and applications. Make a check list of your specifications and go through the latest models ticking off those that best meet with what you want. If that sounds like way too much work for you, there is always the easy way around: make friends with the IT person at your office, or a friend's office, and ask them to recommend a machine for you. That way, you can get what you want with the least amount of effort.

Of course, other than pure amusement purposes, the computer can be used for, yes, work! All sorts of useful software is available to help with accounting, analysis, design, research – the list is endless.

Who are we kidding? Work, shmerk! Everyone knows the REAL purpose of having a computer is to send emails, chat, shop online, join online communities and even find dates.
To do all those things, however, you need one essential tool: the internet.

COMMON TECH TERMS EXPLAINED

- **Bandwidth:** Not a reference to your waistline or belt size, but how much data can be carried by your server or network connection in terms of kilobytes, megabytes, and gigabytes.

- **Download/upload:** Basically, how information is retrieved onto your webpage and what allows you to send information off (like attaching a file), respectively.

- **DSL:** Digital Subscriber Lines, they carry data over your phone line but still allow you to use your phone freely.

- **Kbps/ Mbps/ Gbps:** No, not the name of a new snack food, but the speed of downloading or uploading in kilobytes, megabytes, or gigabytes per second.

- **Modem:** The whatchamacallit that transmits data between your computer and the internet.

- **PDA:** These doohickeys are known as Personal Digital Assistants, like palm pilots.

- **RAM/ ROM:** Types of memory on your computer, but let's be honest, who really cares about the specifics?

- **Wireless distributor:** The thingamabob that distributes the internet connection to the rest of the computers in your home (the computers must have a wireless connection).

- **World Wide Web:** Seriously, you don't know what this means? Stop what you're doing and hitch a ride to the 21st century ASAP!

THE CONNECTION is made

Also known as your lifeline to the world, the internet hookup is the most important installation you will get for your home. In Lebanon, technology is not exactly the most up-to-date, but at least we have DSL. Gone are the days of the horse-and-buggy style dial-up connection, which took forever – waiting for a page to load was more frustrating than missing the sales at Aïshti. You can get DSL from just about any of the internet providers in Lebanon, and even through the phone company, Ogero. Subscription fees depend on the amount of data you want to download per month and the download speed. DSL is the best way to set up an internet connection, no doubt, because it's fast, affordable and doesn't take up the phone line.

Getting to know you... AND EVERYONE ELSE

Once you're hooked up, you will most likely become an addict, especially when faced with the endless possibilities of what you can do online. Let's start with emailing, the communication tool of choice for the majority of the modern world. Admit it, without sending or receiving emails on a day-to-day basis, you would be lost. Nothing compares to the disappointment of checking your inbox and finding it empty! But before you start singing, 'nobody loves me,' click on your address book and drop a line or two to some of your buddies just so that you can see that new message icon light up on your screen!

Then there is online chatting. Can you remember the last day when you didn't log onto your favorite instant messaging program? Some people (and you know who you are) are so hooked that being online is an absolute necessity to get through the day and they can't even contemplate working on a computer if the online chat icon doesn't appear in the bottom right side of their desktop display. The advantages of chatting are numerous. First, and most obvious, is being able to get a hold of friends and family all over the world at any time as long as they are online at the same time as you.

And thanks to the nifty status bars, you can really get detailed information on what your friends are up to - 'out to lunch,' 'having a bad hair day,' 'in desperate need of a manicure,' etc., and even what music they are listening to at that moment.

The second useful function of chatting is being able to send files and pictures in an instant by merely clicking on the name of the online recipient with your mouse. It surely beats the lugubrious method of attaching files to an email like they did way back in the dark ages. Third, and perhaps the most serious of the functions, is communication among work colleagues in different offices, either in the same location or across the globe.

In fact, you can always use communication with other employees as an excuse with your boss so that you'll be granted access to online chat programs. Be sure not to abuse this privilege, though, and spend the time gossiping with the person in the office next door about the unfortunate nose job the receptionist got over the weekend!

TEN WAYS TO SPOTTING AN ONLINE CHAT ADDICT

1. They're always smirking while typing on the computer, even at work.

2. They quickly change what's on their computer screen when someone walks in (also applies to pervert downloading what they should not be downloading).

3. They laugh hysterically to themselves.

4. Their typing skills have improved exponentially from one word per minute when they got their computer to 110 words per minute a week later.

5. All communication is done through chatting.

6. They start talking in chat speak – saying, 'lol,' instead of actually laughing out loud.

7. The extent of their writing abilities is limited to chat abbreviations – e.g. 'cu,' 'thx,' 'brb,' etc.

8. They take their PDA or cell phone with them to the bathroom so they can chat literally at all times.

9. Their faces start looking like chat emoticons.

10. Whenever the internet is down, they start to look like Amy Winehouse's song *Rehab* was written about them.

Are you FACEBOOKABLE?

If you're not a member of one online community or another then you had best join one now before you start feeling like a social outcast. From MySpace to Facebook, these virtual neighborhoods are the social hubs of the millennium, and chances are most of your friends are already members. In Lebanon, the most popular by far is Facebook and anyone who's anyone has an online profile.

Why is Facebook all the rage? For the incredibly vain Lebanese, the answer is simple: the pictures! With the ability to upload albums, complete with captions, and share them with everyone on your friend list and beyond, it's a wonder that it was actually an American Harvard college student who came up with the concept.

Word of warning, though, whenever you're out with your friends and someone whips out a camera, be sure that the pictures are Facebookable, because they will surely end up online the very next day.

Facebook has other incredibly useful functions too. How else are you supposed to stalk your friends? You can literally discover pretty much everything that they're up to, have been up to and will be up to. That is not to mention the endless number of applications that are available, from sending talking electronic greeting cards to playing poker with other Facebook members, including those on your friend list. Profiles even include books you've read or are reading, and the same applies to music and movies. In fact, there's absolutely no need to go out on dates anymore in order to get to know people, since all you have to do is log on to their profiles.

Like everything in life, there are even drawbacks to Facebook – believe it or not. You would think that privacy would be one of these concerns, but since you can always limit who sees what (like only the cute guys getting access to your photos), that issue doesn't seem to be affecting members much. The disadvantage in question is of a far more serious nature – namely, the catastrophe of being seen in the same outfit twice. With all the photographs available to nearly everyone on your friends list, they will all see the clothes you've been wearing out, so you can't wear them to another event that will be Facebooked, or even to another event to which anyone on your list may be attending. This is definitely a sober matter to take into consideration!

Looking for MR. ONLINE

Although quite a risky undertaking, many single Lebanese are turning to the internet to find a love connection. To avoid the pitfalls of ending up on a date with El Creepo, follow these helpful hints for online dating.

1. **Pick a known dating site:** Don't take a chance with a site you've never heard of. Better yet, stick to one recommended by someone you know and trust.

2. **Perfect profile:** When signing up for an online site, make sure your profile is unique and honest. No point in saying you're a Pamela Anderson look-alike when he's going to figure out the truth as soon as you meet in person. If you're being set up via email, remember that honesty is the best policy.

3. **Exchange photos:** Don't bother saying that looks don't count, because we all know they do. Make certain you know what you're getting yourself into by asking for his picture. Sure, he could always send a fake, but chances are if he sends in a photo of Brad Pitt, you're going to get just a wee bit suspicious.

4. **Go with the phone:** After exchanging a few emails or chatting online, move on to the phone to give you that transition phase before you meet in person.

5. **Lower your expectations:** Don't expect to feel an instant love connection with the guy the first time you meet face-to-face. See him a couple of times before you judge whether you want to pursue the relationship or not.

6. **Stay safe:** The first time you meet an online guy in person, make sure it's in a public spot and take your own car. If you don't feel comfortable once you've met him, go with your instinct and leave.

CALLING OUT around the world

Around the globe, the saying goes, 'never judge a book by its cover'; in this country, it should be, 'never judge a person by their cell phone.' Unfortunately, everybody does anyway because nothing spells 'the in-crowd' clearer than the type of mobile you carry. The Lebanese love affair with cell phones began at the dawn of the mobile – no sooner had they hit the market in the '80s than everyone was doing everything short of selling internal organs to afford one. By the '90s, they were the accessory du jour, with just about everyone owning one.

If you have the latest cell phone on the market, you need to show it off in the best possible light, but you don't want to appear tacky and have it hanging around your neck like some sad imitation of a bling-obsessed rap star.

Showing off, after all, is a Lebanese art form, but it has to be done right - subtly and with class.

Follow these helpful hints on how to use your phone as an accessory, letting all around you see your fabulous new mobile without going overboard.

TACKY	CLASSY
Whipping out a cell phone and putting it on the table as soon as you're seated at a restaurant or café.	Making pleasantries with others at the table when seated, then apologizing and saying you're waiting for an important phone call (an office emergency works best) and placing the phone innocuously on table.
Walking around the gym with a cell phone as you work out.	Coming into the gym while already on the phone looking earnest, so that everyone thinks you're merely being polite not cutting someone off in mid-conversation. When you hang up, sigh and look a little miffed that you have to lug your phone around with you.
Talking on the phone while at the movies.	Bringing out the cell phone, but just to turn it off, taking your time so it can be adequately admired.
Answering the phone while visiting with friends.	After chatting for a while, apologize and say that you need to make a quick phone call to so-and-so about something inconsequential that sounds serious. Talk on the phone for a maximum of two minutes, and then casually leave your phone out afterwards, but make sure you don't answer any phone calls while you're there.
Answering or bringing out your phone during a work meeting.	See cinema entry above.

Now that you know how to elegantly present your phone to the world, it's time to figure out how long before an upgrade is required. There is no requisite period of time for changing your phone, however, as a general rule, if the buttons are still big enough for you to push comfortably, you need a new one. (Unlike most things in life, when it comes to mobiles, the smaller the better!)

Picking a phone is relatively easy, because all you have to do is choose one you like within your budget range. When shopping for a new one, look for a brand that's in the news, preferably a new model that's creating a lot of buzz and one that has a waiting list. The fact that you got yours before most other people will only elevate your status as a phone fashionista.

MUSIC to go

In this day and age, every respectable Lebanese girl should own an MP3 player, without question. Whether in your car, at the gym or even while running errands, listening to your tunes of choice has become an absolute must if you have any kind of musical taste whatsoever. Imagine, you can 'walk the line' with Johnny Cash and rap along with Kanye West with the simple push of a button. Genius! Remember, though, as with cell phones, size does matter, so pick a brand and model that is as slim and light as possible. A cool and funky color is also a nice touch – remember this is yet another technological device that can serve as a fashionable accessory within your social circle. Also important is your choice of playlists. You don't want anyone to get a hold of your MP3 player and discover that you're a closet Englebert Humperdinck fan. You might as well buy a one-way ticket to Timbuktu if that happens.

Of course, that is not to say that your playlists should not reflect your own musical taste – taste being the operative word – but just keep the selections as non-cheesy as possible. For example, if you're in the mood for light listening, skip Humperdinck and opt for Sinatra.

GUIDE TO CREATING THE PERFECT PLAYLIST

1. Upload all your CDs onto your MP3 player library of choice.

2. Separate the songs in your library according to genre and year – e.g. '80s pop' or '90s Alt/Rock'.

3. Usually, information about songs, such as album and genre, will upload automatically from your CDs or when they're downloaded legally; if not, though, do it manually.

4. Rate your songs so that you can group your favorites and separate them from tunes that are still growing on you – this is especially useful if you're not quite sure whether or not you like a song.

5. Come up with original playlist names like 'Having a bad day' (alternative music), or 'Feel good and drive' (pop music).

6. If you're limited by memory space on your MP3 player, change around your playlists often so that you don't get bored. Remember, if you delete it off your device, it'll still be available as part of your library on the computer.

Chapter XI
Haute Garage

Road rules

Female drivers in Lebanon are always getting a bad rap, but as long as they're seen in the latest Beemer or Range Rover, they don't seem to care. In fact, the first step to driving in Lebanon is getting the right vehicle – the more expensive, the better. Just imagine the embarrassment if, while standing with your friends waiting for your car to come back from the valet, a no-name patchwork of metal came rolling around and the keys were handed to you! Scandalous indeed.

Society girls know that anything less than luxury spells social suicide,

so it's better to go hungry for a few months to buy the hottest wheels of the year than to be seen in public driving anything less.

In most countries, the next logical step is getting a driver's license, which includes driving lessons and a test. However, many women in Lebanon don't worry about tiresome matters such as the rules and regulations of driving and will instead use *wasta* (connections) or any other means possible to skip on the lessons and get someone – usually a dad or husband – to get them a driver's license without taking the test. Although it is not advisable to miss this all-too-important phase – maybe more drivers would know what they were doing if they clocked in a couple hours of drivers' education – the typical Lebanese lady does not trouble herself with such burdensome details, especially considering the driver's test has to be conducted in an archaic stick shift. Everything today is automatic, so why shouldn't the process of getting your license be the same as soon as you hit 18?

Now, when it comes to actually getting on the road, you should have some idea of what you're doing, if only to protect your shiny new set of wheels. Driving here should not be like a chase scene out of an action movie. Everyone knows that driving in Lebanon is crazy, but you can do your part to make the streets safer by actually staying in a lane and signaling when you want to change lanes. Believe it or not, those white lines drawn on the roads are not just decoration – they are there for a reason, so try keeping your car within them.

Also, although courteous driving seems to be non-existent among both male and female Lebanese drivers, it's okay for you to break out of the mold and actually drive according to the laws, at least the basic ones. This includes stopping at red lights (yes, red means stop), giving right of way (kind of tricky, but in general, cars on main roads have right of way, which means, if you're on an intersecting road, you stop and let the other car pass), and letting pedestrians (people that actually walk) cross the street once in a while.

Another helpful tip is to keep calm in the face of road bullies, who think it's the ultimate driving sin to pass them and, therefore, make it a point to purposely block you if you dare try.

Men usually see a woman behind the wheel and, all of a sudden, 'thou shalt not overtake thy neighbor's car' becomes one of the Ten Commandments.

Men will be men and you are not Evel Knievel, so don't even bother engaging in road combat with such ignoramuses, no matter how tempting.

So now that we've covered the car, the license and the know-how, it's time to tackle a topic of extreme importance: accessories! Here are the top four that any respectable Lebanese woman should possess before even thinking of going behind the wheel.

1. Sunglasses Be sure to do your research on the latest 'in' style before you make your purchase. You don't want to be caught in aviators, for example, when oversized are the fashion. A clear designer logo along the brow or on the handles is a big plus, especially since they will be visible to all onlookers on the road.

2. MP3 player Gone are the days when CDs in the car were the ultimate sign of technological sophistication in a motor vehicle. Today, most new cars have an MP3 hookup already installed, and what better way to show off your great taste than with the coolest sound system around (most appreciated by passersby when driving with the windows down). Plus, there's no need to carry around those bulky CD cases that can be an eyesore, because virtually your whole musical library can be stored on these tiny babies.

3. Phone You are always on display, even when driving so don't be caught gabbing on a démodé mobile! (Disclaimer: this is not an endorsement of talking on your cell while driving, which is technically against the law. But, if you are absolutely pressed to make an emergency call – to your manicurist – it's best to have all your bases covered.)

4. Handbag A designer bag should always be placed in the passenger seat so that it is clearly visible from the window (although beware of purse snatchers on mopeds and always keep the doors locked). If – heaven forbid – you're carrying a no-name purse, hide it under the seat because you never know who will pull up beside you and discover your shameful fashion faux pas.

Once you've studied these essential steps and followed them exactly, you will be ready to face the obstacle course that is the Lebanese road system. By the end of this checklist, your driving technique may still be a little lacking, but at least you'll look marvelous behind the wheel!

Fully LOADED

Car maintenance for the typical Lebanese woman is about as foreign a topic as mapping the human genome. Ask her about the basic concepts – such as changing tires, checking the oil, etc. – and you will probably get an amused raised eyebrow, accompanied by a mocking, 'are you serious?' facial expression. Anything remotely mechanical involved with the car, after all, is left for the guys (which is one of the main reasons we keep them around anyway). So, how do Lebanese women handle their average car upkeep?

Changing tires
If you ever see a woman in Lebanon changing a tire, pull over and ask her where she's from, because she definitely will not be Lebanese.

When a Lebanese woman gets a flat, all she has to do is step out of her vehicle and let the guy with her do all the work.

If she's alone, she merely has to whip out her cell phone and call any one of the multitude of males in her life – from boyfriend, daddy to cousin or brother-in-law.

The inconvenience of the wait is nothing in comparison to ruining your nails and getting your hands dirty.

Plus, there's a lot of physical effort involved, with bending and lifting the car up with the jack and using a wrench to get the hubcaps off and removing the tire and putting in the new one and… oh, just thinking about it is exhausting!

Pumping gas
In Lebanon, no one pumps their own gas, not even men. All you have to do is roll down your window and tell the gas station attendant what kind of gas you want and how much you want to spend. If only everything else in life were as uncomplicated!

Checking the oil
Although one of the least complicated aspects of car maintenance, there is no need for a woman to perform even this easiest of tasks. Any gas station attendant will be more than glad to take care of it for you in exchange for a small tip.

Pumping the tires with air
Same as above.

Filling water for the engine and the windshield wipers
Same as above.

Filling coolant or anti-freeze
This task can also be performed by a gas station attendant, but don't forget to actually buy the product.

Oil change and car service
Taking your car in for an oil change and basic servicing is an annoyance for any woman, because you have to take your car to the dealership (using just any no-name mechanic is simply unacceptable for your luxury wheels). Unless the dealership is prepared to give you a loaner while your car is being worked on, get someone else to take it in for you (see "Changing tires" above for more details).

Car wash
Getting your car washed may seem like an ordeal, especially for a busy gal with a full work and social calendar, but being spotted in a dirty vehicle is almost as bad as being caught taking public transportation. So, be sure to keep your wheels spotless at all times, even if it means – do not pass out from shock – taking it in yourself (since some of the major shopping malls have car washes in the parking lots, it really shouldn't be too arduous a task!).

So, is there at least one aspect of vehicular maintenance that the Lebanese woman is expected to perform completely on her own? The simple answer: nope! Believe it or not, there is one silver lining to life in a patriarchal society. How sweet it is!

WHAT YOUR CAR SAYS about you

Ever wonder what sort of signal you're sending out to the world with the kind of car you drive? Here are some of the most popular cars for women in Lebanon and what they say about the person behind the wheel!

IF YOU DRIVE A(N)…	YOU ARE MOST PROBABLY…
Audi	Career-oriented but like to spoil yourself with nice, but not overly ostentatious, material things that you proudly paid for yourself.
BMW (sedan & SUV)	A classy dame with good taste, although a little spoiled and a little pampered… and not ashamed of it (so what if daddy bought the car?)! You are certainly proud to pull up in a shiny Beemer, but do not overly obsess over your image.
Cadillac (sedan & SUV)	Family-oriented, with an appreciation of the finer things in life. You put comfort before your image, but realize that a little luxury goes a long way in this society.
Jaguar	Married with a rich husband and want people to know it. You wouldn't be caught dead in a non-luxury car, even though you drove a beat-up, second-hand VW bug before you hit the jackpot with Daddy Warbucks.
Jeep Cherokee	A working woman with career goals, you don't like to live beyond your means, but don't want to live life in the shab lane either. You are comfortable in the happy 'median.'
Jeep Wrangler	Adventurous and single, with an outgoing personality and a penchant for mischief. You do things your own way and don't really care what others think.
Lexus SUV	Classy yet sensible, with a refined taste for luxury but the wisdom to not over-indulge in the swankier things in life.

IF YOU DRIVE A(N)...	YOU ARE MOST PROBABLY...
Mercedes (sedan & SUV)	A woman with an old school sense of style. You stick to timeless fashion classics and are confident enough to avoid getting sucked into the latest fad.
Mini Cooper	Running with the right people, but reflecting the hipper side of the BMW crowd. You like being original and much prefer shopping vintage to looking like a copy of the typical designer-clad Lebanese Barbie doll.
Nissan or Toyota sedan	Someone who has little use for name brands. You care about functionality and practicality and could care less about the car you're in as long as it has four wheels and an engine.
Nissan or Toyota SUV	More concerned about finances than your car's fancy hood ornament. You are not into flashy status symbols and want comfort that you can afford.
Porsche Cayenne	Married with a rich husband, image is everything to you. In fact, the mere thought of taking public transportation gives you nausea.
Range Rover	Used to the best life has to offer, you want your car to show your high-ranking status in society so that you don't have to overtly shout out, 'Hey, I'm rich!'
Smart Car	No-nonsense, practical and hardworking. You're either still a student or just joined the workforce – either way, you're eager to make your mark on the world and don't really care what car takes you there.
Volvo (sedan & SUV)	A mom with kids, so buying the safest car is more important than buying the most exclusive set of wheels.
VW (sedan & SUV)	Young with a spunky spirit and a knack for picking out the hottest trends. You are always *à la mode*, but with an independent streak that sets you apart from the rest of the crowd.

Chapter XII
Let's Get Physical
(Not That Kind Of Physical)

To diet, or not to diet

Imagine a world where you and your girlfriends can enjoy a guilt-free, fat-aplenty lunch at one of your favorite cafés, including dessert. A world that possessed some type of magical technology whereby all the calories in the most popular junk foods were eliminated, so that no matter how much you ate, in effect, you ate nothing at all! Okay, that probably will never really happen, but a girl can always dream!

In reality, every Lebanese woman has probably been on a diet at one point in her life or another. In fact, many have probably been on diets since puberty. You don't need anyone to tell you that diets are not fun (understatement). Garfield probably said it best when he proclaimed, "Diet is 'die' with a 't', " on the ubiquitous fridge magnet that has comforted dieters around the world for years. The problem in Lebanon is that finding a fat woman is about as common as going through the day without traffic.

In fact, when trying to slim down for the all too important bikini season, many Lebanese women tend to feel like the lone survivor on Fat Island.

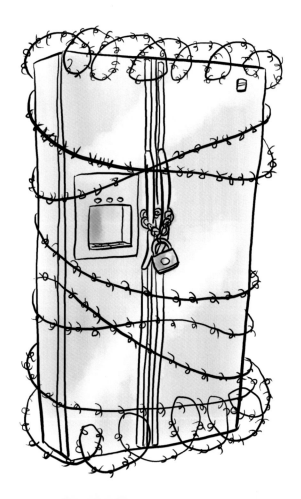

Okay, so admit it, you're not fat *per se*, but you like to exaggerate so that everyone around you can enthuse over how thin you are and how you absolutely don't need to lose a single gram. It's probably just those last two kilos or so that you put on during the winter that you want to shake off so that you can pass the ultimate test and once again fit comfortably into that one item that is both a woman's greatest joy and disappointment: a pair of skinny jeans! And that is what has compelled you to embark on this most treacherous of journeys, the end of which arrives only when you can slip them on without having to lie flat on your back for an hour engaging in a tug-of-war with the zipper.

Whatever your reasons for losing weight, remember to stay away from fad diets at all costs, no matter how many kilos they promise you'll lose within minutes! If a diet sounds too good to be true, then it is. Losing weight fast is never healthy, especially when you have to go to extremes, like cutting out carbohydrates or just eating soup for every meal. If you go for an eating plan that basically requires you to starve to death, you know you're going to cheat and have lasagna for dinner anyway, so you might as well lose weight the healthy way. Going to extremes, even for a short period, just doesn't work because once you go back to your regular eating habits, you'll put that weight right back on again. If you think about it logically, you'll realize

a deprivation menu is plain insanity because in the long run, how is any self-respecting girl supposed to live without chocolate and French fries, *forever?*

If staying away from the *knafeh* and *baklawa* (Lebanese sweets) is just too hard for you to do on your own, salvation is at hand. You can always do what health-minded people across the country are doing and have your meals delivered to you from any one of Lebanon's nutrition and diet centers for as long as you need to shed the pounds. A meeting with a dietician will get you an eating plan designed just for you and will ensure that you lose weight healthily and while eating right (you even get dessert!). This is also a great alternative for anyone who thinks cooking involves a phone and takeout menu, or those who are more familiar with the drive-thru of Burger King and McDonald's than their own kitchen.

Another great way to keep from overeating is staying busy. They say that idle hands are the devil's playground – and for a dieter that is particularly true, especially if the devil in question is cake! A lot of people eat out of pure boredom, so pick a distracting activity that you can use to replace junking it. Easier said than done, right? Well, when desperate times call for desperate measures, just envision your end goal: you, skinny jeans and zipping up while standing upright.

What's in your FAVORITE FOODS?

Everything you wanted to know but were too afraid to check.

Food	Portion	Calories (kcal)	Fat (g)
Baba Ghannouj (eggplant dip)	1tbsp	35	3
Baklawa (sweet pastries)	25g	100	5
Falafel (fried vegetarian patties)	1 oz	60	4
Fatayer (spinach pies)	1 oz	85	6
Fattouch (salad)	100g	180	11
Fried Kibbe (meat dish)	1 oz	60	8
Hummus (chickpea dip)	1 Tbsp	25	1.3
Kafta (meat dish)	1 oz	56	3.3
Kibbe Nayye (raw minced meat)	100g	176	7
Knafeh and Kaaki (type of cheese on specialty bread)	200g (knafeh +1 medium kaaki)	950	25.5
Labneh (yogurt)	1 Tbsp	21	0.5
Maamoul (dates)	25g	80	3
Malfouf (stuffed cabbage rolls)	90g	100	3
Ma'loubet Batenjen (eggplant and rice dish)	350g	410	17
Moujaddarah (lentils)	150g	220	5.5
Shish Kabab (meat on skewer)	1 oz	55	3
Shawarma Djeij (chicken platter)	1 oz	70	4
Shawarma Lahme (beef sandwich)	1 pita bread	400	15.5
Sfiha (dough pastries stuffed with meat)	100g	110	7.5
Tabbouleh (parsely salad)	100g	150	12
Tahini (sesame seed sauce)	1 Tbsp	90	8
Toum (garlic sauce)	1 oz	185	19.5
Warak E'nab (stuffed grape leaves)	10g	20	1.1
Zaatar Mankouche (thyme sandwich)	180g	558	19

Source: Nadeen Massaad, Nutritionist and Dietician

Getting BOOTYLICIOUS

Gym culture in Lebanon is like no other. In general, the goal of joining a gym may be to get in shape, but in Lebanon, it's where many get to show off their latest Juicy Couture tracksuit and ability to gab on the phone while working the treadmill without breaking a sweat. Being able to say you belong to one of the swankier gyms – sorry, health clubs – in town is a social must – it's almost as important as the kind of car you drive or the designer brand of your handbag. Although membership to a gym has become mandatory, actually stepping foot in one is optional.

If you do decide to take advantage of the membership (you've already paid for it, so why not?), be sure you're well prepared. You don't want to make the disastrous mistake of showing up wearing your significant other's baggy old t-shirt and boxer shorts – *quelle horreur*.

Remember you are NOT there just to workout. This is Lebanon, where even your sweatpants have to be designer.

After you've picked the gym du jour, head out to the mall and pick up a new wardrobe of assorted designer gym wear. Make sure the label is written in huge letters somewhere visible (preferably right across your rear so people can read it while you're on the treadmill). As long as you get the brand name right, anything goes as far as colors and styles are concerned, but make sure you have enough outfits so that you won't be seen in the same gear twice in the same week – *quelle catastrophe.*

Your brand of tennis shoes is just as important as your outfit, especially because logos are printed loud and clear across the sides. Your footwear must absolutely appear shiny and new at all times – scuff marks are tantamount to you being compared to a bag lady! Finish off your gym look with nifty accessories, including the latest MP3 player (remember that clip-ons are so '90s, and opt for the much more fashionable armband to carry it around in). Gym accessory *numero uno*, however, is the water bottle. Forgo the local brands and go with something European, preferably French. Last, but certainly not least, is the cell phone (goes without saying).

Now that we've covered clothes and accessories, it's time to discuss hair and makeup. The disheveled look is a no-go in any situation in Lebanon, including the workout. If you must break a sweat, try to be as inconspicuous about it as possible. Many Lebanese ladies have taken to carrying around a little vanity bag (designer, of course) as they workout so they can readily apply touchups to the face and hair when needed. If you can't exercise and keep your look together at the same time, then this is a good option for you.

It's not a good idea, however, to look overly done up, so unless absolutely necessary, avoid using foundation – you don't want your face to come off on your towel after wiping down. When it comes to the hair, a simple and elegant ponytail or messy bun is the best way to go. It may take you a while to get it just right, but at least it'll look like it took you seconds. If you appear overly coiffed and made up, you run the risk of looking like you're auditioning for an adult film.

There is a fine line between looking well-groomed and looking like a Pamela Anderson wannabe (you want to go for the former, not the latter!).

With the look down pat, it's time to consider the attitude. You can't just walk around the gym as though you were window shopping at the mall. No, you must acquire the Lebanon Gym Strut. Don't panic, it's not too difficult to master: first, practice your facial expression in front of the mirror so that it shows just a hint of a smile, a touch of disgust, a dash of sexy, topped off with a whole lot of confidence.

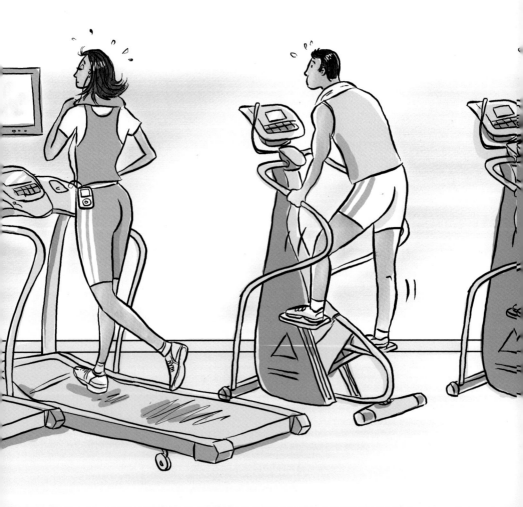

Be careful not to go overboard on the confidence because then you'll just end up with a face full of snub-nosed superiority. Second, comes the walk. Try a little coquettish sway as you peruse the various machines – look like you know what you're doing and actually use one once in a while. Do not lumber around like one of the walking dead; be spry and have a little oomph in your walk. You are at the gym after all!

Getting the right look for the gym is a workout in its own right. But, if you still have energy afterwards, you could try to actually exercise.

GYM MANNERS

Some helpful hints on how to mind your manners even when at the gym!

- Don't reserve machines while you go off to get changed or chat with friends.

- Remember to wipe off machines after you've used them.

- If there's an obvious wait for a treadmill or bike, don't stay on for longer than 30 minutes.

- If someone is waiting to use a machine you're on, offer to take turns in between reps.

- Never stay on a machine talking on a cell phone, especially if someone is waiting to go after you.

- Wait your turn if there is a line for a machine.

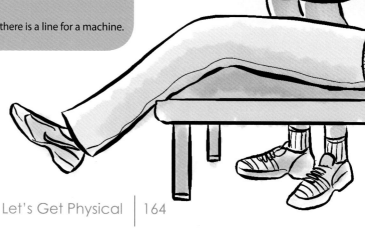

THINGS TO DO AT THE GYM OTHER THAN WORK OUT

If working out is not on your agenda when going to the gym, there are other activities you can partake in to while away the minutes!

1. The 'oh my goodness, look what she's wearing' fashion show.

2. The 'talking on cell phone while on the treadmill' acrobatics.

3. The 'please don't mess up my hair and makeup' workout.

4. The 'oh my God, I'm sweating' panic attack.

5. The 'look her up and down' stare-down contest.

6. The 'dab the sweat without messing up makeup' arm lift.

7. The 'casually let hair loose to show off tresses before putting back up in ponytail' routine.

8. The 'weightlifting in front of mirror so can look at self without appearing vain' workout.

9. The 'offhandedly adjust tracksuit to showoff sculpted abs or legs' reps.

10. The solely for men, 'who can grunt the loudest' weightlifting competition.

FITNESS finesse

Thanks to the fitness craze that has taken hold across the country, you do spot genuine health-minded women at the gym, working out and seriously getting into shape without paying any attention to the rules of popular gym behavior. If you count yourself as one of these ladies, then grab your sweats, put your hair in a ponytail and get yourself to the Stairmaster pronto!

If you're new to a gym, be sure to first of all ask one of the trainers to show you around and instruct you on how to use the machines. The hi-tech treadmills can be kind of tricky (especially when it comes to operating the attached TV screen!). Although sliding off the treadmill or bike can look charmingly funny in the movies, in real life it's just plain embarrassing and you could do without being referred to as 'the chick who fell flat on her face' on your first day.

A good way to work out and look ultra cool in the process is to hire a private trainer (and if he's hot, all the better!).

> One advantage of having your own trainer is that he or she can also provide other bonuses, like getting the details on the yummy guy with the tattoo who comes in everyday at 7pm.

Your workout guru can give you his stats – status, height, weight, body fat content, etc. – and even introduce you if the opportune moment arises. That's not to undermine the professional trainer's ability to give you rock-hard abs and a rear that would even make J.Lo jealous – but, it's always good to know about the fringe benefits!

If you're more into group classes to get you into shape, most gyms offer a really diverse program. Here are some of the most popular classes at Lebanese gyms and the benefits they offer.

CLASS	BENEFITS
Aqua aerobics	Taking place in the pool, the aerobic exercises are low-impact, putting less stress on the joints, but effective because they use the resistance of the water.
Oriental dance	A fun way to burn calories and get your abs in shape – plus you learn some great moves in the process.
Pilates	With a focus on strengthening core muscles, this class uses specific localized exercises, along with balance and breathing techniques to shape the body.
Spinning	A hardcore fat burning session that will get your lower body in tiptop shape.
Tae bo	A truly sweat-inducing high impact session, involving 'cardio-boxing' and a multitude of aerobic moves to work out the whole body.
Toning	Focusing on certain body parts – abs, glutes, legs – each class concentrates on specific muscles to sculpt and shape.
Yoga	There are several forms of yoga – including the more relaxing Hatha yoga and the more intense Ashtanga yoga – but the basic principles of breathing, stretching and balance to tone the body are the same.
Yolates	A combination of yoga and pilates, this program also uses breathing and various movements to increase your overall strength and stamina.

Chapter XIII
Mind Your Manners

Path to politeness

Under the word 'courteous' in *Webster's Dictionary*, you will find one of the definitions listed as 'marked by respect for and consideration of others.' Seems easy enough, right? Unfortunately, in Lebanon, the word seems to be lost on most people.

Well, ladies, here's a newsflash: It's okay to be polite.

In fact, in some cases, it's actually encouraged. If you're ever confused about when to extend courtesy to others, the below is a brief outline of eight main rules of etiquette – a how-to guide, if you will, for how and when to mind your manners according to the situation at hand.

1. Waiting IN LINE

This is one area where consideration works wonders. There's nothing more annoying than waiting in line to pay for something while shopping, only to have some heathen with the manners of a barnyard animal push in front. It's just plain rude. This popular trend is particularly visible at boutiques on the weekend and while waiting at the box office at the movies, where people take standing in line to mean forming a 'chaotic amoebic blob.' It is not a pretty sight. At times, crowds are so aggressive, you need the skills and gear of an American football quarterback in order to get through a line unscathed, complete with play strategy and maneuvers all mapped out.

Waiting in line should not be such a stressful ordeal. Your turn will come, eventually so what's the point of acting like a caveperson when you could get there just the same by conducting yourself like a lady?

If everyone around you is pushing and shoving, do not follow the 'when in Rome' rule. Simply tell any obnoxious offender to wait their turn and point out that there is a line. After the initial look of shock, they are always shamed back to the end of the line. If a store clerk starts serving a person who has pushed in front of you, politely point out that you were next, and they will almost always oblige.

People who cut in line are not being clever, they are being rude and that is nothing to be proud of. There is always the courteous and discourteous way to do things and, universally, it's always best to opt for the former.

2. Saying 'PLEASE' and 'THANK YOU'

These are probably the two most important words when it comes to manners. They're also easy to pronounce in Arabic, English and French, so there is no excuse for not using them when appropriate. It's a good idea to be an equal opportunity 'please' and 'thank you' person, which means exchanging these two words with anyone who does something for you, including housekeepers, wait staff and valets (yes, they are people too).

A good time to say 'please' is when you're in a crowded area and you want to politely step in front of someone in your way. Unfortunately, people here prefer to physically shove you aside rather than go to the trouble of uttering that simple, one syllable word. (NB: In this situation, feel free to also use the phrase 'excuse me' in any language of choice.) You should also say 'please' when requesting something from someone. For example, 'Can you hand me the latest issue of *Vogue*, please?'

As for 'thank you,' there are countless situations in which the phrase is fitting. Generally, one should utter those precious words when something is done for them. When a waiter brings your order or when someone pays you a compliment are both prime opportunities to show off your impeccable manners. If saying the two words seems like too much trouble, you can always go with the simpler and shorter 'thanks' – it gets the job done in half the time!

3. DRIVING

The lack of courteous driving in Lebanon is a time-old problem, so where does one begin? Don't cut people off, don't get angry when people overtake you, thank drivers that let you pass when you don't have right of way (learn the meaning of 'right of way'), don't roll down the window and shout out obscenities, etc. In fact, the intricacies of driving in Lebanon are such that they deserve a chapter on their own, so for a complete breakdown of driving courtesy, see Chapter XI.

4. At the MOVIES

Talking during a movie is a Lebanese phenomenon that drives most audiences insane.

Why bother to spend money on a ticket (maybe even popcorn) only to chat or gossip on the phone when that can be done anywhere else for free?

It may sound crazy, but some people actually like to watch the movie they've paid to see. Legitimate movie goers in Lebanon often suffer through countless encounters with irritating, inconsiderate types sitting in the theater, chatting away as if they were in a café – nothing could be more frustrating.

There are actually several different types of movie talkers. First, there are those who 'predict' every move the main characters are about to make, like 'Oh, now he's going to open the door,' or 'Now she's going to blink her eyes,' etc. Very useful indeed, because stating the obvious is always necessary when watching a film. Second, we have the 'lost in translation' crowd, which consists of those who feel obliged to translate every single word of dialogue to their date or companion, subtitles in both Arabic and French not being sufficient.

Last but not least, we have the potpourri mix of cell phone gabbers, gossipers, loud eaters (yes, chewing popcorn with the mouth closed is an option) and high school teeny boppers who find it absolutely hilarious to scream inane comments at the screen.

The above is certainly enough to keep any avid film fan away from the theater, but you can make a difference by being considerate, and staying quiet and turning your cell phone off. Let the actors do the talking – it's really not very complicated, so go ahead and give it a try the next time you're at the movies.

5. SMOKING

Unfortunately, smoking is endemic in Lebanon. If you don't partake in this particularly nasty habit, you are in the minority. For some reason, the 'thank you for not smoking' attitude that has taken over the world has somehow missed this tiny corner of the planet. Pretty much anywhere you go is filled with clouds of smoke from various forms of tobacco: cigarettes, cigars, pipes and the traditional *nargileh*. With the abundance of smokers, it is no wonder that the considerate Lebanese smoker is pretty much non-existent.

For non-smokers, having smoke blown in your face when you're trying to enjoy a meal is very off-putting, to say the least, especially in confined spaces. What is more annoying than sitting at the sushi bar only to have the person sitting next to you puffing away? You end up inhaling second-hand smoke instead of your sashimi. What's even worse is when you go out with freshly washed and styled hair only to come home smelling like an ashtray.

Ladies, for you smokers out there, please (notice appropriate use of manner rule number two) exercise some consideration the next time you decide to light up in front of others.

It is not okay to smoke in the presence of non-smokers without asking if they mind. Believe it or not, the world does not revolve around you – shocking but true – so ditch the incredibly unflattering princess attitude and make a slight effort to extend some courtesy to the people around you.

6. Table MANNERS

It has been said that the test of a true relationship is being able to watch your significant other eat without being disgusted. This being the case, it is absolutely remarkable that the divorce rate in Lebanon is not higher. It seems that most Lebanese don't even know that table manners exist. Well, they do and are incredibly important to incorporate into your day-to-day eating activities. Here is a brief refresher course for those who have forgotten how to be courteous during a meal in an easy, step-by-step tutorial (for those in the know, use these tips to enlighten your less refined dining buddies).

Here are the basic concepts of table manners for beginners in a nutshell!

- As soon as you sit at the table, place the napkin on your lap. If you have to leave the table before the meal is over, place the napkin on your seat. When you've finished your meal and are ready to leave, put the napkin on the table.

- Elbows off the table as long as food is present.

- Don't start eating until everyone on the table has received their food.

- Use the appropriate cutlery according to the course being served – i.e. salad fork and knife for salad, etc. It's really not hard: start on the outside and move in. When you're done eating, place the fork and knife side by side at four o'clock on your plate. For soup, place the spoon on the plate – never leave it in the bowl.

- Don't pick your teeth with a tooth pick at the table. On that topic, don't reach for the sugar packet and pick your teeth with that, either. After the meal, head to the bathroom and take care of any food-stuck-in-teeth problems.

- Most importantly, do not talk with your mouth full. We do not need to see the start of your digestive process – that is just nasty!

7. BUYING gifts

Most Lebanese consider being called stingy the ultimate insult, which is why gift buying can be such an ordeal. In this country, deciding on the budget rather than what to buy is the most strenuous task.

In general, the rule of thumb is to spend however much the person you're buying for spent on you, give or take a few dollars. For wedding presents, the trend nowadays is just to deposit a lump sum, either at a bank or a specific shop listed on the 'liste de mariage' (wedding registry). In such cases, it could be a little embarrassing to put in less than a certain amount, so be sure to stay within the 100,000 Lebanese pounds (LL) to $100 range, even for those you're not that close to. Of course, with close friends and family, the amount goes up, depending on your relationship, so be prepared to spend the big bucks.

Yes, reputation is everything - and a good one will cost you a pretty penny!

8. Being CHARITABLE

Speaking of generosity, it's also a good thing to spread the wealth to the less fortunate once in while. Keep in mind that you don't have to wait for a specific religious event to give to the poor, especially if they are out on the street selling something, or if they are disabled and obviously unable to earn a proper living. If you can afford to buy those Manolo Blahnik shoes, you can certainly spare LL1,000 for a pack of Chiclets and help out a person in need. You could also try donating your time and volunteering with any of the admirable charitable organizations in Lebanon.

Generosity is not always about money and you will definitely feel a lot better about yourself if you sacrifice that massage or facial to help out someone else instead!

Chapter XIV
Getting Away

Ready to go

One great thing about Lebanon is that it feels like you're living at the center of the world. So, if you're in the mood to go shopping crazy in Milan, get romantic in Paris, or become a beach bum in Thailand, it's no problem – your desire is only a plane ride (or two) away! Even if you're just bored and want to discover an exotic new locale, it's a wonderful feeling to get away from the everyday doldrums and explore someplace new.

Not surprisingly, however, a major drawback to modern day traveling for the average Lebanese person – even if they have a foreign passport – is

aggressive security checks that make you feel like you have 'I love Osama Bin Laden' tattooed on your forehead.

Going through countless searches and interrogations can really take the joy out of traveling and make you feel like you would've been better off staying home and watching reruns of *Star Academy*. But, when going through an airport ordeal, just remember that it will be short-lived and you will likely forget all about it when you get to where you're going!

To be considered part of the elite crowd, however, you must brave airport security and embark on at least one vacation per year to a fashionable hotspot. Since some Lebanese live under the illusion that they are European, it should come as no surprise that the holiday country of choice is – wait for it – France, of course! It doesn't necessarily have to be a fancy holiday, it just has to *sound* fancy – e.g. if you had a one-hour layover in Paris on your way to another, less desirable destination, you say that you stopped over in the French capital to shop and then lunch on the Champs-Élysées (sometimes, all it takes is flying over the country to say that you've been there).

As a finishing touch, when you get back to Beirut, pretend that you've forgotten how to speak Arabic and start rolling your 'r's with a French accent, even if you've never actually been to France.

Best of both WORLDS

If you don't have the time to go abroad, but are in need of a break, you could always head to a local getaway. It's actually the best of both worlds, because you get a vacation without having to go through the hassle of traveling. You also have a lot of options – from mountains to beaches, Lebanon pretty much has it all!

For some ideas on where to go, check out the table below.

IF YOU WANT TO...	HEAD FOR...
Relax in the sun sipping cocktails while getting a tan and then take a refreshing dip.	One of Lebanon's many beaches, where you'll be greeted with sun, sand and good times. Some of the beach resorts in the north and south have beautiful bungalows where you can spend a delicious weekend, or longer, by the sea!
Ski and snuggle with a mug of hot chocolate during a cold winter.	The ski resorts in the mountains, where you can stay in luxury accommodations. Most Lebanese ski towns also have great restaurants and nightclubs so that you can have a blast in the evenings as well.
Hike, camp or take in the country's beautiful eco-tourism.	A nature retreat with any of the local activity organizers. Your experience could include nature hikes, rock climbing, camping and a number of other activities taking place in the great outdoors.
Pamper yourself.	Any one of the country's deluxe five-star hotels that offer spa treatments and so much more, either in or out of the city. Turn off the phones, order room service, and enjoy!
Eat, drink and be merry.	The Bekaa Valley and tour Lebanon's wine country. Stay in a hotel in the resort town of Zahlé and then visit a different vineyard a day, tasting wine and enjoying a scrumptious meal surrounded by beautiful greenery.

In for the LONG HAUL

If you're going on a long haul trip for at least several weeks, getting there is really a hassle – especially with layovers and changing terminals and sitting in a plane for hours on end. And, before all that, the preparations are one big stress fest, complete with getting passports and tickets in order, finishing up projects at work, and paying bills, to name but a few. But, perhaps the most tiring part of traveling is packing, especially for ladies who need an assortment of outfits, shoes and accessories. For some helpful tips on how to get you, yourself and your luggage ready for the next time you travel, read below!

- Don't buy fancy luggage – this is probably one of the only situations where you should never buy designer – so that thieves won't be tempted to swipe your suitcase.

- Pack clothes that mix and match so you get several outfit changes while taking up minimal space.

- Shoes are bulky, so try and bring two to three pairs (two casual and one fancy) that will match all your outfits.

- Don't take anything overly personal in your hand luggage, since you will most likely be searched and your items paraded in front of onlookers. Also, don't put in any loose cash, as it'll be easy to steal – and always, always keep an eye on your stuff when being searched.

- If you're traveling alone, it's best not to bring a large carry-on that you have to lug around without any help.

- Always bring a snack for the plane journey because you may get the munchies before or after a meal is served, or you may not like the airplane food (surprise, surprise!).

- Never wear foundation – the high altitude dries out the skin, and a lot of makeup will make it worse.

- Get your hair done right before you travel so that your locks will be easy to manage during the flight. This is especially important if you're going on a long journey and likely to sleep – you don't want to wake up looking like you stuck your finger in an electric socket!

- Don't get a French manicure because you will unavoidably be using your hands a lot and the tips are the easiest things to chip.

- Always pack an extra pair of socks in your hand luggage, even if you'll be given a courtesy toiletry bag on the plane. Wear your socks underneath, with the airplane socks on top. Remember, bathroom floors on planes contain 'splashes' from people with poor aim or because of a bumpy flight, so unless you plan on putting shoes on every time you need to use the restroom, double up on the socks!

Here comes THE SUN!

One of the best parts of the much celebrated Lebanese summer is going to the beach! But, if you think all it takes to go to any one of the country's private beaches is a bikini and some sunscreen, you would be so very, very wrong.

Becoming a true Lebanese beach bunny is a process - there are rules, regulations and, most importantly, removal - as in hair!

Well, maybe getting beach-ready is not all that serious, but there are certain steps you must follow if you're going to hit the golden sands in style.

BODY pump

Lebanese women are beautiful, and nowhere is this 'fact' clearer than at the beach, when teeny tiny bikinis reveal them in all their glory! With nary a cellulite rear in sight, you'll feel like a beached whale if you don't firm up and get those thighs and abs ready for exposure, and not just to the sun! (For more details on how to get in shape, check out Chapter XII.)

Wax ON, wax OFF

Of course, it should come as no surprise that an essential part of beach preparation is heading to the beauty salon and making sure that all traces of unsightly body hair are removed. Whether wax, sugar or laser, just make sure that you won't be mistaken for the shaggy dog when you hit the shores. (For more details on grooming, see Chapter I.)

BIKINI hunt

One of the most traumatic experiences in a woman's life is going bikini shopping – yes, it is that bad. Most women, even those with great bodies (bitches!), have a hard time stripping down to the bare essentials and parading their various body parts for all the world to see. In fact, buying a bathing suit is probably one of the only times that shopping is not fun, because all you can think about are flabby thighs, big butts, small boobs, soft tummies and protruding love-handles.

If you think a bikini is too revealing and you need the coverage offered by a one-piece, think again. Wearing a one piece is only okay if you're the sporty type and swim laps at the gym. To fit in with the rest of the bathing beauties at Lebanon's beaches, only a bikini will do. Do not fear the two-piece! With some careful shopping and a good eye for what looks good and what should be delegated to the rag pile, you will find a suit that makes you look like a supermodel (or at least close to one).

Part of the problem of finding the perfect bikini is knowing what looks good on your body type. Thanks to modern technology, a good suit today can give you cleavage where you have none, make your legs look longer and even hide less than rock hard abs. Plus, most shops sell tops and bottoms separately so if you're not exactly proportional, it'll be a lot easier for you to find a bikini that fits.

For more of an idea of what cuts suit certain figures, check out the table below.

BODY TYPE	THE CUT
Bootylicious	Sir Mix-A-Lot famously sang that he liked big butts – no lie – and Jennifer Lopez made them famous, so if you're blessed with a large posterior, learn to flaunt it in the best light. The most flattering style for you is bikini shorts. Warning: do not buy anything with a skirt unless you're 80.
Buxom	A large chest is the envy of every woman who was ever teased about looking like an ironing board when she turns sideways! Alas, the lucky ladies in this category need never worry about that happening to them. To highlight your assets, choose a bikini top with under-wire support, so that you never droop or have anything pop out unintentionally!
Cleavage seekers	Great things come in small packages, so don't fret about needing a little extra help in the cleavage department. Go for a bikini top with padding, or one that ties at the neck to lift and give the illusion of fullness.
Average abs	Okay, everyone wishes they had washboard abs that didn't flip flop with every step they take, but not everyone has the stamina to do 1,000 sit-ups a day and not eat. So, for the everyday gal who likes her *chocolat mou* and *biscuit au chocolat*, try wearing a tankini top (a bikini top styled as a tank) to cover your soft spot.
Daddy long legs	If you fall under this category then be prepared to have every other woman hate you, because you can pretty much wear any bikini style there is, especially the sexy, barely there, string tie bottoms!
Petite princess	So you don't have long, supermodel legs – big deal! You can still look hot in a bikini by choosing bottoms with a high cut to make your thighs look longer and slimmer.

ACCESSORY advisory

When going to the beach in Lebanon you must be seen carrying the right accessories. It goes without saying that designer sunglasses are a must! When it comes to the beach bag, of course, luxury always works better, but no one is going to deny you entry if you show up carrying something without a known name. Anything goes for a beach towel, but for your own comfort, make sure that it is long enough to cover the whole chaise longue. A hat is always a cute fashion accessory that also doubles as extra protection against the sun. Plus, it has the added benefit of covering up frizzy hair after a swim! One must-have, however, is the *paréo,* or wrap-around skirt, which absolutely has to match your bikini. You should use these wraps every time you leave your sun bed, even if it's just to take a dip in the pool (in which case, you drape it poolside while you swim). Next on the list is footwear, another area in which designer names are a plus rather than a necessity. You don't want to look like a fool in fancy heels walking poolside when a regular pair of flip flops will do just fine, and suit the occasion more appropriately.

Hair and MAKEUP

Most women would laugh at the idea of styling their hair and wearing makeup at the beach, but this is Lebanon, where most women would laugh if you didn't.

Try to keep things low maintenance, though, so that you don't look like your face has melted off because of the heat or water – i.e. use water-proof products! Lipstick is a no-no, because it's just too obvious – the key is to look good and natural at the same time. The same applies for hair: nothing froufrou, but giant frizz balls are definitely out of the question.

There's no point in going to the hair salon just to go to the beach because the humidity and swimming will wreck your 'do in no time. But, you should still style it yourself – a sleek ponytail or trendy hat are great ways to keep locks tame and fashionable.

TANNING essentials

A great tan is one of the most coveted features of stylish Lebanese women, but you don't need to fry your skin to get one. When exposing yourself to the sun, remember to always protect yourself by using a sunblock with at least SPF 15, especially on your face. Self-tanning products from just about every major beauty line will guarantee you great color without the risk of premature aging, unless you're okay with having wrinkles before you hit 30! The colors are natural looking and most products guarantee streak-free results. For smooth, evenlooking color, exfoliate before you apply.

Other sun-free options include tanning beds, which are convenient for many women on the go. One major drawback to this option, though, is that you're still exposed to harmful UV rays that will really damage your skin. A safer alternative that won't prematurely tap into your fountain of youth is spray-on tanning, which is offered by some beauty as well as tanning salons. Remember, it's a lot easier to add some color to your skin than it is to get rid of wrinkles!

No matter where you decide to go for your vacation, whether in Lebanon or abroad, you will undoubtedly be constantly reminded how lucky you are to call Lebanon home!